Bear in Mind

Stories of the Troubles

compiled and edited by

An Crann *The Tree*

Lagan Press / An Crann *The Tree*

Belfast

2000

Co-published by
Lagan Press
7 Lower Crescent
Belfast BT7 1NR

An Crann *The Tree*
10 Arthur Street
Belfast BT1 4GD

ISBN: 1 873687 13 3
Author: An Crann *The Tree*
Title: Bear in Mind
Stories of the Troubles

Cover: *Redeemer* by Carol Graham
Design: December
Set in Garamond 9.5/10 pt on 12/13.5 pt
Printed by Noel Murphy

Funded by the European Regional Development Fund

Because what is forgotten cannot be healed,

and that which cannot be healed easily

becomes the source of greater evil.

Lionel Chircop

Acknowledgements

An Crann *The Tree* and the publishers would like to thank the following: Harry Brandsma, Averill Buchanan, Paul Campbell, Janet Davidson, Dave Duggan, Mary Gordon-McBride, Damian Gorman, Carol Graham, Jane Harrison, Maureen Hetherington, Brenda Hill, Gráinne Kelly, Evelyn Kinloch, Kirsten Lavine, Katy Radford, Susan Salters, Damian Smyth, Natalie Strain, Sara Wengerd, The staff at: Clondermont High School; Enniskillen Collegiate Grammar School; Integrated College, Dungannon; Lenamore Primary School; Mount Lourdes Grammar School; and Saints and Scholars Primary School.

Special thanks to The European Regional Development Fund, administered by The Community Relations Unit, especially John Carson, Irene Garrett, Kathleen McKernin and Dennis Ritchie. We would also like to thank the staff at The Community Relations Council, Mark Adair, Patricia Heffron, Stella McDermott (now with Heritage Lottery), and Jenny Shaw for previous funding for writing workshops which contributed to the production of this book.

Most importantly, we would like to thank the contributors who gave so openly of their own experiences.

Photographic Acknowledgements

An Crann Archive 1997 Photographer Unknown – Page 2; Belfast Exposed – Page 16, Page 23, Page 31, Page 100; The *Belfast Telegraph* – Page 6; Harry Brandsma – Page 24, Page 62, Page 65, Page 113; December Publications – Page 34; Lesley Doyle – Page 11, Page 14, Page 41, Page 61, Page 76, Page 86, Page 96, 106; Lizzie's Family Archive – Page 5; The *Irish News* – Page 51; Gráinne Kelly – Page 45; Northern Ireland Tourist Board – Page 119; Pacemaker – Page 19, Page 26, Page 29, Page 55, Page 58, Page 67, Page 71, Page 78, Page 128, Page 134; The Scott Family Archive – Page 93.

Carol Graham

Carol is a Northern Irish painter who currently lives and works in Lisburn. A student at Cambridge House School in Ballymena, she went on to study Fine Art at the Art and Design Centre, Belfast. Paintings produced in her early career as a painter were mostly representational in character and she completed quite a number of portraits, including James Galway and Dr. Mary Robinson. During the early 90s Carol suffered an emotional crisis which led to her painting in new styles that have been described as symbolist. The painting 'Redeemer' is part of a large collection of work completed over a seven year period and exhibited in both Belfast and Dublin as 'Into the Darkness, Toward the Light'. An Crann invited Carol to share her thoughts and feelings about her work, and how it was affected by her difficult emotional experiences:

> "The collection 'Into the Darkness, Toward the Light' came out of the deepest, most prolonged period of depression in my life. Working through this time creatively, was often frightening, yet wonderfully revealing, empowering and healing. Initially fearful, I probed the darkest recesses of my psyche, and in learning to see and accept what society regards as the negative aspects of character, I also discovered so much of value – hidden treasures.
>
> "I also discovered the paradoxical strengths and vulnerabilities of myself as a woman, while simultaneously realising and expressing my innate spirituality. As a long-term agnostic, this was very challenging, but felt very meaningful. 'Redeemer' is one of these images."

Carol Graham
March 2000

Foreword

Bear in Mind is a remarkable book. It is also a disturbing one, expressing an infinite variety of raw emotions and sensations and a broad spectrum of wildly differing opinions and viewpoints from many whose lives have been deeply affected or scarred both physically and mentally by the civil strife of the last thirty years or so in Northern Ireland, a state of affairs which, like other similar periods in our recent history, we have chosen to call *The Troubles*. Alas, this most recent and most prolonged spell of violence has left its mark on several generations of our children who have grown up knowing nothing else, and whose parents' lives have been darkened by sectarian divisiveness and suspicions.

Leaving aside the simplistic divide that takes into account only the polarised, confrontational extremes of unionist and nationalist politics, equating them respectively and arbitrarily with anyone and everyone from Protestant and Catholic backgrounds, a unique aspect of this collection is that it appears to consist of largely unedited first-hand stories from *all* sides of our community, including members of the police and emergency services who are involved as a matter or course in every crisis, stand-off, and disaster; a squaddie returning to the scenes of his soldiering has an interesting tale to tell, as has a Chinese boy subjected to racial and religious harassment; but above all, it is those who have suffered personal loss and been closest to the carnage, or who have lived with personal involvement, threatened or actual violence, and direct confrontation, that have most need to talk – "a massive need", as one contributor puts it, "to be able to talk about what has happened to them." The contributions themselves range from the banal, through the poetic, to the sensationally riveting eye-witness account of the Omagh bomb and its unspeakable aftermath. Yet each and every story, with its share of love and hate, bitterness and recrimination, enmity and suspicion, forgiveness and reconciliation, has something of value to tell us. The fact that these diverse and tragic aspects of our common problem appear side by side between the covers of a single book is a thing of value in itself, and may hopefully point the way for the democratically elected members of our rather unstable assembly, who must learn for all our sakes to share a common roof.

If true democracy consists not so much in government *by* a majority *for* a majority, as in government of, for, and by the people, then all views held by each and every member of our power-sharing body must be freely aired and discussed, without the threat of bomb and gun, or indeed any other form of coercion. That sensible statesman and orator Edmund Burke declared "A state without the means of some change is without the means of its conservation." If a change of heart ensures the conservation of our hard won peace, then surely that change is worthwhile. Respect for the culture and religious faith of our neighbours becomes increasingly vital as we, like so many parts of Europe and the larger island across the Irish Sea, become a multi-racial and multi-cultural community. The monster Ignorance must be put to flight and bigotry and suspicion replaced by tolerance, openness, and, above all, by wide-ranging knowledge and liberal education. Voltaire, another eminently sensible fellow, had this to say about knowledge, whilst at the same time taking a side-swipe at near-sighted sectarianism:

"It implies a strange mental narrowness to love one branch of knowledge and hate all the others; we should leave that fanaticism to those who believe that it is not possible to please God except in their own sect."

If this book helps to show the futility and essential ungodliness of sectarian hatred with its all too frequent recourse to violence, if it opens eyes to what we share in common as distinct from what divides us, if it demonstrates, however painfully, that the only way forward now is to live and work together in a quest for lasting peace, for the sake of our children, and our children's children, then the enterprise will have been worthwhile. As for the contributors themselves, many of whom have been manifestly damaged by their physical and mental involvement in the violence, it is to be hoped that the shared experience of producing such a work will prove a sound catharsis for the sweetening of bitterness and the softening of sorrow. At all times it should prove to be an essential source book for students of our tragic conflict. May the lessons to be learned save lives elsewhere.

James Ellis

Introduction

In the following pages, over seventy people give voice to their experiences of the troubles. The medium through which they speak varies, as do their experiences and their responses to them. What unites each of the contributors is that they have a story to tell and have chosen to share it.

It might seem odd that I use the word 'story' when even a quick glance at the book reveals a diverse range of literary forms. Around one third of the contributors to this volume recorded their story orally with An Crann *The Tree*, and in consultation with those people, extracts were selected from their taped interviews for publication. These extracts can be identified through titles which form the first line of the text. In the other two thirds of the book, people speak through various prose styles, poetry and even drama. These pieces were gathered by An Crann through writing workshops conducted over several years, or gathered in response to an open invitation for contributions to the book in Autumn 1999. I call them all 'stories' because they are all forms through which people attempt to find meaning and order for their experience and memories, and, in essence, that is what a story is. It is the structure through which we describe and explain our experiences, both to ourselves and other people. Through stories or narrative, we try to make sense of our lives and the world around us.

What makes sense to one person, however, does not necessarily make sense to someone else because what we remember and how we remember it is influenced by our values, beliefs and aspirations. One's recollection may be different to, even incompatible, with another's. Within the covers of this book there are a lot of conflicting stories. An Crann *The Tree* hopes that such fragmented, contradictory stories of the troubles can be respected through being heard. This is a difficult challenge, because stories are often hard to hear. They may touch our humanity very deeply through their sadness and tragedy, or our sense of justice. Because they also have the power to shape our perceptions of ourselves and others, an openness to them can confuse our preconceptions and assumptions, forcing us to give up some of our self-images, beliefs or prejudices. There are many reasons not to listen if we are afraid of change.

Despite the challenges, and maybe because of them, I hope you find the time and the openness to read this collection. There is a wide range of voices in this book, although it is by no means 'the last word'. As a society coming out of a violent political conflict, we are just beginning to reflect and talk and it will be many years before people overcome the fear and lack of confidence to speak. Some might never, and we will only get to hear their story through their silence.

I pay tribute to all those who have taken part, some of whom have shared very personal and painful experiences. It is in acknowledgment of their hurt and of those who have sadly died, that we borrow the words of the poet John Hewitt to name the book *Bear in Mind*.

Cathie McKimm
Director, An Crann *The Tree*

Bear in mind these dead
I can find no plainer words.

The careful words of my injunction
are unrhetorical, as neutral
and unaligned as any I know:
they propose no more than thoughtful
response.

John Hewitt

Contents

Bomb Scare

I remember the time I was in a bomb scare in West Side Stores. My friend and I were in Lifestyle, so we all ran out. I phoned daddy to collect us and he came.

Sometimes I wish I lived somewhere else.

Paul, aged 11

Four Bombs

The first bomb I was close to was when I was working for the *Irish Times* in Belfast. We had an office in Lombard Street – two rooms in an old building over a fashion store called Petal, which has long since moved elsewhere. We were on the first floor above the shop, and above us was the *Cork Examiner,* represented by Walter Ellis. One evening he rushed into our office and told us that as he was coming into the building a man had parked a car right outside the front door, about a yard out from the footpath. He got out of the car and just walked away, leaving the door open.

We immediately rang the police, who said they had heard nothing. However, as we were discussing what to do we heard an English voice outside, yelling through a loudspeaker for the street to be cleared immediately.

There was no way out except through the front door past the bomb. The only alternative was to go to the back of the building and pray, and none of us felt like putting our trust in God at that particular moment. We left the building hastily one by one.

As I was going out of the front door, only a few yards from the car with the door open, one of my platform sandals fell off. As I groped round desperately with my toes trying to get my foot back into it, Martin Cowley, who was right behind me, told me to leave it. He grabbed my arm and hauled me hobbling one-shoed up the street and round the corner to safety.

I remember my spine prickling as I waited for the bomb to go off behind us and blow us to smithereens.

I got my shoe back half an hour later – after the bomb exploded and blew it up to the end of the street. I found it among the rest of the debris, miraculously unscathed – unlike our office, which was wrecked. If we had stayed in it we would have been killed or badly hurt, prayers or no prayers.

Jill

Three Generations:
Mother, Daughter &
Granddaughter

Ena It was before the war, the first war – you'd have been about 12, mummy.

Lizzie Yeah, I would have been about 12.

Dale And where did you work, granny?

Lizzie I was working in Smithfield. I was a weaver. Wove cloth you know, my sister and me. We got chased out of work. When we came out into King Street that day, there was a crowd waiting for us with sticks to beat us. One girl that worked with us had long hair. When we came running into Gresham Street, there was four fellas trailing the girl along Gresham Street by the hair. She had a big head of hair. And I shouted to them, all the height of me. Four fellas beating one girl. When we came round into North Street, they were firing at Carrick Hill. We got into a shop door where they boxed tea, and the door opened and a young fella brought us in and shut the door, because they were shooting at Carrick Hill. They thought they'd let us stay there till it quieted down – then they let us out. We went up over Peter's Hill, and as we were walking up Peter's Hill, I met your daddy coming down. He worked up in the foundry in the Springfield Road and he got chased too, and put out of work. We were only going together at the time.

Ena I remember the day your granny had us all up at Carlisle Circus on the twelfth of July. Do you remember that, mummy? We were standing there and my granda,

Lizzie, who died on 13 November 1999, shortly after recording her stories with An Crann The Tree. She was 97.

your great-granda, was the sort of person that when he left the Master's Lodge, he didn't give a damn if they threw the biggest bomb, my granda would have said, "I'm going back. I left from the Master's house and I'm going back to the Master's house." He wouldn't have took his sash off for nobody. The next thing, we heard the shooting and a wee fella was shot dead. It was his first day walking with the Orangemen. They'd opened fire on the Orangemen coming from the Field. Do you remember, mummy?

Lizzie I do. The wee fella Charlie was shot dead. That was his first day to walk. They fired out of the big pub on the corner of Donegall Street.

Ena Yeah, but they were firing out of the chapel too. My daddy's lodge was already up and my ma, she was screaming her head off, "Oh Tommy, where's my da?" and your granny was shouting, "Oh Tommy, where's Alec, where's Alec?" And my ma's away like hell looking for my granda and there's firing out through St. Patrick's chapel in Donegall Street. The Orangemen couldn't get into the chapel or they'd have wrecked it. I can remember all this and I was only a child at the time.

Lizzie Our Maureen, the youngest, was only in a pushchair.

Rioting in York Street, 1930s

Ena It's a long time ago, mummy. I'm 72, so you're talking 65 years at least. I'm only a year and ten months older than our Maureen, so I would have been five. I'll never forget it. It was an awful day. My dad couldn't get my granda out of it. He'd gone to Upper Meadow Street to the Master's house and he wouldn't come out, sure he wouldn't, mummy? My granda was terrible. He wore his bowler hat and all. He was a real Orangeman, in the Black and everything. He didn't give a hoot. He just walked on. He's a small stout man, and he just walked on. He was so proud of it, so he was. Your granny always says, if he was here now, he'd get things settled up at Drumcree. He'd go down to the Garvaghy Road, he

would. He's mustard, or he *was* mustard like. But he was very, very loyal where the Orange and Black was concerned. So's my daddy. Do you remember Uncle Albert, mummy?

Lizzie Aye.

Ena He wouldn't have missed a parade – he wasn't a one day Orangeman, he was an Orangeman every day. That's what he used to say. He wouldn't have missed it, even if it had been snowing he would have walked. He was in the B-Specials and all. The B-Specials. They were fantastic so they were. If they had let the B-Specials do the job when these troubles started, if they'd let them do it, because they knew everyone, and it was only a small minority, a small group, if they'd let them do it, there wouldn't have been all this trouble today. Do you remember the morning, Dale, I was in work in the laundrette at ten past and couldn't understand why no-one was there?

Dale I do. I'd have been about 14 the day you're talking about, still at home. It must have been around the late 60s, early 70s. You were at work around the corner from where we lived, and there was a massive explosion.

Ena Two hundred and fifty pound bomb it was.

Dale Only yards from where you were standing.

Ena I was standing at one of the machines and had the second powder needed to go in, I would have walked over and set it on the counter. But next thing the bomb went off and the window was a million pieces – right over the machine I'd just been standing at.

Dale If you hadn't moved, you'd have been killed. I'll never forget it. The sound of a bomb being so close to you like that. The sound of it always stays in your memory. Bloody Friday's another day I'll never forget. I

was 15 and had been working up in Ligoniel. It was my first job. We finished work at one o'clock on Fridays and were walking home when the bombs went off. You could see the town so plainly from Ligoniel. You could look right down and all you could see was these massive explosions and you could see the smoke and that the bombs had all been concentrated in one area.

Ena Twenty-eight bombs went off that day.

Dale The hard part about these things is, for every person who loses their life there's a story. There's always a story behind every death in Northern Ireland. I'm 42 years of age and I've brought my kids up to believe in their heritage and their culture. But at the end of the day, being a Protestant to me is about being loyal. But it doesn't mean you have to be bitter. There's a big, big difference here. I sometimes hate the way the media, when there's a bad atrocity say it's the 'loyalist community'. I hate that terminology because on both sides of the community, there's always a small percentage that want to keep this running. The highest majority in this country, both Catholic and Protestant, wants this to end once and for all.

Lizzie, Ena & Dale

On Friday 8th August 1981, Peter was doing his usual stint as doorman at the Hillview Club. In the course of the night, he met an old friend whom he hadn't seen for a long time. They had a drink, then another, and so on – until he was bleutered. I came into the club and had to tell him to go home as he was making an exhibition of himself. We had a bit of a row and I was hardly speaking to him the next morning.

Peter got up on Saturday, washed, shaved, had his breakfast. Things were still not right between us. He went out to do his job as doorman, came home at 6.00, had his dinner, sat with Louise and Robert on his knee and played with them for a while. He left at 7.30 to go back to the club. He assured me he would not be drinking and we had sort of made up. I went to work in the club at 8.00 – it was a very busy night, as it was the eve of internment, so everyone was getting ready for the bonfires. We both got home about 12.15 a.m. I made Peter something to eat, then I took Margaret – who is my eldest child – up to the bonfire. There were a lot of young people up on the Muck Hill, sitting about drinking and trying to get a sing-song going, so a few shouted over to me to give them a song.

The Worst Day of My Life

I sung a few rebel songs, then we went down the hill and home. We got to the house at 1.15 am.

Then I heard loud bangs. We went out to see what was wrong. The RUC were firing plastic bullets at the bottom of Mill Road. A crowd then came to the bottom of Dandry Street. They were throwing petrol bombs at black taxis and cars travelling along Shore Road. We went out to see and to talk to some of the young lads – I was afraid one of these bombs would hit the tree next door.

Next thing we knew, the RUC came flying in. I was pulled up to the house by Barney Cash. I heard a bang, looked back. Peter was running up the hill, and said, "Bell, I'm hit."

He passed me in the hall, tried to get onto the chair, fell onto the floor, and never got up again.

Someone stopped an ambulance, one of the men came into the house and tried to help Peter. He worked on his chest. I could hear his ribs cracking. He could not do any more for Peter. The priest came – who was my cousin's son and gave Peter the last rites. Peter lay on the floor for about two hours. I went about making tea, because after people had heard Peter was shot, they crowded into my small kitchen. I still had my overall on from the club. Detectives came into my house to interview me. I was talking to them, but did I really know what I was saying?

They left.

The men came to take Peter away – they put him in a black zip-up bag, so I was a long time waiting for him to come back. On Tuesday we had the funeral – people came from all areas.

It was nice to know Peter was so well thought of.

Isabel

Granny's House

I love going to my granny's house, especially when she makes soup. My mummy's soup tastes nothing like my granny's! It is always fun in my granny's house. She is forever carrying on with us. The only time I see her sad, really sad, is on the 13th of May.

My uncle John, my daddy's brother, was 19 when he was shot by the army down in William Street on the 13th of May 1972. My granny and granda were really sad when they heard this, and every year on his anniversary my granny still cries. My granda thought of my uncle John until the day he died. My granny still misses him very much. My daddy was only 13 when it happened. He was out working with the milkman. It was a Saturday afternoon and when the milk-lorry drove into the street where my uncle John lived, daddy knew that something bad had happened because of the crowd of people that were outside his house. Then his cousin came over to him and told him that his brother John had been shot and killed. My daddy's feelings just dropped. He told me it was as if his heart stopped, and he burst out in tears.

I love it when my daddy tells us stories about John. When it comes to John's anniversary my daddy always misses him. John would be 46 years old now. That was in the dark days of Derry. I'm glad I didn't live in those days.

Deirdre, aged 11

Blood & Milk Bottles

I was eight years old. I was wearing a grey poloneck dress with belt and pockets, which made me look even fatter than ever, and I hated it. Funny things you remember.

They must have been Protestants because granny would never have helped Catholics. I knew that. How? Because granny had a Vanguard plaque (plastic, gold coloured) on her living-room wall inscribed with something about 'defending Ulster', and she had also just told Uncle John that if he married Dymphna she'd kill herself. There were also lots of disgruntled murmurings and louder jibes at the television when certain faces came on, and cries of approval when others appeared. Something was going on, but I didn't know what.

They were coming up the road, the Springfield Road, and we could easily hear them inside from the back of the house. The front door was flung open and out we rushed, out to stand at the gate. A few at first, running, sometimes backwards to better see the melee. "Have you a drink, love?" asked one – big, sweaty and shaky. Mummy ran back into the kitchen and filled a milk bottle with water, which she gave to the man. Numbers multiplied, some tripped and fell up the road, others just ran. More came over to ask for a drink.

I was sent in to fill up bottles and bottles. I was frightened by the noise, but fascinated by the excitement, size and energy of the crowd. This was new, different from anything I had ever seen on my side of town.

Hurrying back out, there was the crowd, streaming past the gate, steamy, noisy, yelling. One man was holding his head and blood poured out and down his cheeks and neck. "Give me some," he gasped and poured the water over his head, spreading the blood down onto his shirt. He turned his head and guldered, "Ah, ye black bastards," and I looked sideways at mummy to see her reaction. To my surprise she just craned her neck to see further down the road, round the bend to the police station. They're fighting with the police, I realised – but why would people do that?

It was 1969.

"Go you back in," said mummy, gathering her senses at last. It was too late, of course, for I would always remember those scenes.

Entertainment. Excitement. Bewilderment.

Joanna

I knew something had happened to Brian, I just knew he was dead…

Even my son used to go up to the Glen Road in the morning when it was all fields and hedges and trees to look for his body. That's the way it was. We knew in our hearts that our Brian was dead all along.

He was never well as a boy – he'd be in and out of hospital and had bad asthma and eczema. He didn't grow very much either, and when he was 14, he was diagnosed as having the mind of a six year old child. Brian was the one we were protective of, including the rest of the children. They protected him too. He was very, very popular in the area with the neighbours and was always singing and played a mouth organ. He was very musical, even in school. He wasn't academic, but all the teachers were very fond of him. You always got a laugh out of Brian. He was funny without even meaning to be. Anyway, growing up in a place like Andersonstown, he did get involved in throwing stones at the saracens and that kind of thing. That was all the amusement there was for the kids, but he never joined the paramilitaries.

Things got really bad in Andersonstown and there were a lot of sectarian murders. One night, when Brian was about 22, he didn't come home, which wasn't like him. My husband and I were out of our minds with worry and didn't go to bed that night. We were waiting for the police to come round and say his body had been found because

of a sectarian murder. My husband eventually went out, and he discovered that the IRA had lifted him out of a club over some robbery that had taken place the night before. We'd known nothing about the robbery. After 48 hours of being missing, Brian arrived home in a real state.

I'll never forget the state of him, his wee face, and his jaws were clamped down. He'd been through that much and it showed. He started to tell us that he had got mixed up in the robbery at a clubhouse owned by the IRA. There was seven others and he'd told me the names of the others who were involved. The next morning my husband and I took him round to the clubhouse and paid back his share of the stolen money and made Brian apologise to the manager. We apologised too, saying maybe it was a blessing in disguise and maybe it would teach him a lesson and he'd never get mixed up in anything like that again. As I say, he hadn't much sense, and probably did it to be the big fella, to show off. That had happened on 16th May 1978.

The following week, on the 25th May he was heading out to work. I can still see him that morning among all the fuss, everybody getting ready for work and rushing about and shouting "You near finished in the bathroom?" Anyway, he was a bit late that morning so his sister said she'd drop him off to work. He had his good leather jacket on and I said to him, "Why don't you put another jacket on you son? That there's too good to go to work in." But he said he wanted to be tidy because it was Thursday. His sister came down the stairs and the two of them went out and I remember him turning round and saying, "I'm away, mum, good morning," and the two of them left. That was the last time I saw him.

Everybody came back home for dinner at five o'clock that night. I always had dinner ready at that time. A knock came to the door and when I answered, it was one of Brian's workmates to see where he was. He hadn't turned into work that day. Alarm bells started ringing in my head because Thursday was his pay day and if he'd been dying he would have went to work. On a Thursday night he would have come with his pay, got his dinner, gave his daddy the pound he owed him, Martin the pound he owed him, you know. Paid us all back. When his daddy came home, he was worried as well and got in touch with a man in the area who would have been a Godfather. He said he would find out for us what had happened to him. The next day, Friday, he came back to the house and told us the IRA had taken him and he'd keep us informed. The following Wednesday the man told us Brian was getting put out of the country. I was told not to go near the docks in case there would be a scene when I saw Brian getting onto the boat, and there would have been. I said to myself the first thing Brian would do, would be to ring from whatever part of England he was in.

I stayed up all that night waiting for that phone call to come. I waited all the next day, and the day after that. Every time the phone rang, I was running to it thinking it was Brian. The IRA said now that they didn't have him, but you kept waiting for the phone to ring, and when he didn't phone, I'd be wishing it was the day after, maybe there would be a phone call then. You just kept wishing. Then you were wishing it would be next week and next month. Months passed and there was no word of Brian. I felt that they were beating him, because the time they had him for 48 hours, they had tied him up, hand and foot, and he was lying blindfolded on the floor while they were tormenting him. I could imagine them feeling around his legs to see where they were going to put the bullets in. Then they started putting word out that Brian had been seen in the south at some caravan site. My son drove away down to the site but nobody had seen him. The next thing, he was in France, England, Mexico, all these different places. In the first year I was in and out of hospital. My husband had one heart attack after another with the stress. My youngest daughter, she was just 14 at the time, and to this day, I can't remember who looked after that child. What was once a happy home, loving, musical, laughing turned into the deepest pit in hell. When my husband inquired, he was told to stop asking questions and that's the way it was. Nobody would talk about it where we lived and I felt guilty, like I'd committed a crime. To live among Provies, if you're not for them, you're against them. I took down the Sacred Heart picture I had on the wall and smashed it into a million pieces. I hated God. I hated the world.

Margaret

Every country in the world must have a police service...

and if the community agrees with the law of the land, there's no worry about the police service. The police only acts if the law has been broken. If you have a riot situation, the law has been broken.

Before the civil rights marches in 1969, I could go to any city or house or any place. After 1969, the IRA caused an awful lot of fear in Catholic areas through intimidation so that people there were afraid to talk to police officers. Some of them did talk to you, but they were afraid because of the intimidation. This didn't stop the police doing their duty, then or now. As far as I'm aware, the police go into all areas in the North of Ireland. Sometimes they encounter difficulties going into certain places, but there's no such thing as a 'no-go area'. Somebody may lob stones or petrol bombs or something at them before they get out, but they do go in. They have to. The police have to carry out their duty. They have to go in there. They have to be prepared to go in to do their duty, because it doesn't matter where it is. If something happens, if somebody has a fatal accident or something like that, they still have to go in to get the particulars and take the necessary action. In the case of ordinary crime, the police can do nothing unless it has been reported to them. In the case of serious

crime or injury, that's entirely different. That has to be investigated. If somebody is seriously injured and taken to hospital, we have to investigate, irrespective of whether we like it or not. We can't allow any vigilantes to do the policing, because they haven't any law to back them; they are a law unto themselves. You must not let that happen.

The present police service is adequate and should be accepted. I agree there should be more Roman Catholics. I certainly agree with that, but I doubt if they'll get 50/50 because in the early days, in my early days, it was a third. A lot more Catholics would join if their families wouldn't be intimidated. A lot of Catholic people, if they join, have to do it quietly and not come under notice. That's not easy, to know you're maybe putting your family at risk – your father and mother, brothers and sisters. But to change the name of the police service, I don't think that will make any difference. To change the badge and take away the 'Royal' won't help more Catholics to join. The current uniform is green. You know, Irish is green. It has a harp, which is Irish. It has a shamrock which is Irish. Green, the harp and the shamrock. What more Irish can you get than that?

John

Excommunicate

Mother, quietly damned,
hidden shame,
unspoken pain.

Bans, still widely enforced,
on joining forces
with those armed forces.

Excommunication, anathema,
latterly gave way to
tar and feathers.

Hail Mary, full of grace,
at the hour of her death
you surely showed more compassion,

than that ignorant, bleating priest had
for her, or for her children,
who could not remember their responses.

There have been many loves
on this island
that have dared not speak their name.

Debbie

It was almost Christmas. Coloured lights dangled in the evening darkness and crowds pushed in on me. I was ten. It was the first year that I didn't believe in Christmas, because Santa was only a childhood fantasy, explained away by a caring parent.

We were shopping in the busy Saturday evening crowds and I held tight to my father's hand as he fought his way forward to the sweetie counter. My mother's treat was two ounces of chocolate drops or jelly babies, or whatever inexpensive sweet was on offer. My father, on the other hand, always commanded sweets by the half pound and offered us children a full quarter-pound of whatever delicacy took our imagination. The heavy burden of damp bodies suffocated me, and I laid my head against the soft sheepskin surface of my father's winter coat. Shopping bags skimmed against and about me.

Christmas Memoirs, 1970

"Are we nearly there, daddy?"

He looked down and saw a weary face which prompted him to place me directly behind him while holding firmly onto my hand. He said it was our own horse and trap. I shook his outstretched arm and shouted, "Giddy up," and he galloped his way through the throng, while I kept snugly behind.

We arrived at the counter and he stopped a few feet from its edge and pulled me in front of him, shielding me again from the onslaught of Christmas shoppers. I looked up and could see raindrops glisten on the fur of his Slavic hat. He looked like a Russian soldier. My father laughed and joked with the counter assistant and proclaimed that he had to taste the goods before he could buy. I gazed in wide-eyed amazement as my father succeeded in picking and eating a range of soft centres and toffees without an exchange of money. He popped a fudge square and a caramel-wrapped toffee in my hands, while the girl laughed and weighed our final selection.

It was then I noticed her. She too was fighting her way through the Christmas crowds, but she was fighting her way to us and not the collection of chocolates on the counter.

"Mr. Paisley, Mr. Paisley, I just couldn't pass you by."

She grasped my father's hand, held it tightly and shook it. My father greeted her with his usual Christmas cheer.

"Oh, I can't tell you how much I admire you. Keep up the good work. Well done. God Save Ulster."

"Of course He will," my father said and spoke with her for a few minutes, lifted his hat in a form of salute and bid her Happy Christmas and God's Peace. I stood stunned.

"But you're not Mr. Paisley, daddy."

"I know," he said, "but that wee woman thinks I am, and sure it would break her heart to know I was Seamus Ferguson from the Creggan!"

Once outside we huddled together against the winter cold. Shielded from the evening drizzle by his large black umbrella, we ate chocolate toffee and bon-bons. The evening sky was lit by an array of stars, coloured Christmas lights and the orange glow from the burning effigy of Lundy who swung high above us on Derry's walls.

"Who's Mr. Paisley, daddy? Is that the man on the TV?"

Linda

Stolen Innocence

The car behind me blew like a crisp packet, the contents scattered in pieces. The remains were of an engaged couple on active service. It didn't matter what organisation they belonged to. They were dead, disappeared, vanished. Only bits of their charred bodies remained. Years later, it is still too gruesome to recall.

I was 17, walking home in the seaside town of Newcastle, unaware that this night would be with me forever. It was years before I benefited from a night's sleep and loud noises still cause my body to become rigid.

From time to time, I stop and wonder why they did it – that young couple. They risked everything and lost everything.

I also lost something that night – my innocence – as I realised the savage deeds human beings are capable of in the name of … whatever.

Wilma

You came home, dumped the school bag, and headed for the nearest riot…

That was just the culture of the 70s in the parts of West Belfast and Newry where I grew up. Most of my peers were engaging in riots and street protests and everything else. It was just a daily part of life, almost a routine. This was reinforced by the fact that I came from a very strong, traditional republican family, with involvement in active and physical force republicanism traceable to the 1940s at least. I spent much of the early 70s between Belfast, Newry and Dundalk. This was due to the fact that my father was on the run and we, at one stage, had been intimidated by loyalists. Several members of our family, including my father and brothers, served prison sentences for republican activities. Again, where I grew up this was not an unusual thing as many other families experienced this and worse. I also had a brother murdered as the result of a personal dispute under the cover of a so-called 'republican' feud.

In my late teens, I developed a strong sense of political awareness which led to my involvement in activities which at the time were undervalued or ignored by republicans, i.e. CND, supporting the miners' strike, health and other state cutbacks. This was during and after the hunger strikes and anyone leaning towards left-wing politics was viewed with suspicion. However, in retrospect, these were difficult and menacing times. Around this period I

became deeply impressed by the works of Connolly, Lenin, Marx and others and was drawn towards socialism. I saw no contradictions at that time with supporting the republican struggle and advocating socialist politics. I often look back at these times and cringe, but you can't rewrite the past. I regard all those years of political involvement as one big learning process. And despite the harassment, discrimination and other hardships that I have endured, my experiences have made me a strong and principled individual.

I can understand why I was attracted to working in the community sector in the mid 1980s. I suppose it may have been a substitute for political involvement. The political developments of the past six or seven years have turned republicanism upside down and inside out. I think this has been a positive and necessary development, as republicans needed to modernise their strategy. Most other shades of political opinion have embraced change, although some are still stuck in the past. Despite an uneasy peace, the North of Ireland has become increasingly polarised; this is one of the unpleasant results of the ceasefires. If the imperfect peace lasts beyond this summer, then I believe that political violence will fade into the wilderness (with those who support it).

I know what cold metal feels like when you hold on to bars and press your forehead against the cold shape. I remember it because it happened more than just once. It is a weird, an uncomfortable memory, but it does not scar my mental well-being. What I was watching hasn't maimed me either. In a cruel way I have benefited from it.

Everything was usually coloured grey, as it normally happened at night. I don't remember bright, romantic moonlit scenes. My attention was on the arguments down in the hall at the front door. I would crouch looking through the metal banister bars at the scene played out below. My mother would plead, beg and order my father not to go. He would plead, explain and state that he had to go. The men at the door would say little. What they did spit sounded alien to me, their words were that steeped in fear and arrogance. I was glad not to see their faces. I felt no curiosity for that. My parents and the men at the door struggled to whisper. Each person tried to squeeze as much emotion and power into hissed words as possible.

Only my father was lucid. He would explain again how he had to go. He had sworn to. It did not matter who was hurt, or who they had hurt in the process, or for what reason. He had sworn to treat all. I knew then more of the Hippocratic oath than any doctor I have met since. This reasoning drowned in my mother's despairing, loose-cannoned mind. The gun pointed at my father's head held no appreciation for such high morals either. The two at the door knew to point it at him as this had the most leverage. He had no thought for himself, but she was unpredictable. Point at him to control her, the unknown. It was as simple as that.

When these self-made heroes had dragged my father

A Door on the Troubles

off, my mother was left alone on the floor of the hall, each quiet sob deflating her more. With a strength I can still only dream of, she lifted herself up and went to the kitchen to sit on a hard wooden chair and wait, suffering a tiredness that doesn't let you sleep. I sneaked back to bed. The quietude of the event had been for my benefit. I did sleep. At the age of seven, I did not know not to. I didn't wake to hear him get back, but he was there in the morning, as always.

Guns have never struck me as political or religious. It never seemed to matter who or what you were; they just pointed at you with the same devoted monocular attention, despite their obvious disinterest in whom they were about to puncture.

Some time after, I stood at the same door looking at several rifles pointed in. My mother was the strength again this time, as my father was at work. There was a beating-up of a man at a checkpoint. His wife, with child in one arm, was trying to pull them off her husband with the other. My mother had pretended to take a photograph of proceedings. Spotted, we were immediately surrounded by the soldiers. I remember being impressed by the way they had run up the hill and jumped up a wall that I was too small to jump down. They had banged on the door to recover the suspected camera. My mother had the entrance plugged, with herself and her seven children, me included. Her only weapon was the ability to speak clearly and precisely, affecting a slight upper-class English accent. The confusion was obvious. These soldiers had been trained not to question officers so one began speaking like an officer. It was as if the fox had got hold of the horn. I can remember the real officer arriving and demanding the camera. My mother, eventually, admitted the camera to have been a paperweight poked through the blind. He decided to give us the benefit of the doubt and not beat his way past to search the house. Even his sense of justice, his gracious gesture, recalled the night-time visits; for I could not tell the difference. A gun is a gun, and I have yet to see the dead march.

Enda

My whole life changed...

when I was 15. My father was killed by a drunken driver when we lived in New Barnsley, off the Springfield Road. Just after my father was buried, there was a cross put in the door, and we were told to get out by the Catholic community. I had five brothers and two sisters and my mother was suffering a nervous breakdown after my father's death. We moved back onto the Shankill again, and I swore revenge against the Catholic community, joined the paramilitaries and became involved in serious crimes.

In 1977, I was arrested and charged with murder, and attempted murder of a ten year old child. When the car came round the corner two men opened up on it and the ten year old was in it. The gunmen didn't see the ten year old child. No matter what I say now, I cannot bring those people back or bring that man back. If words could bring them back, I guarantee to you now, I would bring them back. For these things, I got life imprisonment.

When I look back, it's senseless, because the hatred and bitterness that I had was just a one-way ticket. Back then, I wasn't really worried what happened to me as long as I got revenge on Catholics for what they'd done to my family. I just pray to God that some day, I might be able to meet the people I've hurt and give them an apology for the heartache I put them through.

Four years ago, I gave my heart to the Lord and I now have a love in my heart for all Catholics. I have no hatred, only love towards Catholics, no matter who they are – republican, Sinn Féin, ordinary Catholics. My door's open for anybody. I have a heart of love. Sometimes the children I work with will come to me and say, "But you were a bad man before. My daddy told me about you," and I would sit and talk to them and tell them that I was in darkness and hatred and bitterness then, but it's not there anymore.

I don't believe that Christians are doing enough for the people. Church doors close on a Sunday night and don't open until the next Sunday. There's still queues that's walking the streets and saying on a Monday, "Wish it was Sunday and I could see the pastor or the priest." On the eleventh night I was at a party on the Shankill Road. It was on a Sunday night, and a Christian lady condemned me and said, "You should have themins in church," and I says, "Listen, if Jesus was to come to Belfast tonight, would He be sitting beside you in the church? He'd be on the streets with the people, because that's where the people's hurt." What's the point in walking down the road with my Bible under my

arm and there's people committing suicide, people on drugs, alcoholics, people murdered, marriages busting and I'm not worried because I'm okay and my wife's okay? I believe we should be on the streets, because Jesus lived on the streets. Let's be real with people and not false. I'm all for being real.

Society is corrupt and I believe, personally, that it's getting worse and we're in the last days, that the world's coming to an end. I believe it because I've never seen so much homosexuality – two gays going to adopt kids and they're holding hands and standing in the street. Years ago you never heard of it. There's a lot of single parents. You look around and there's young ones that's 15 pushing prams. It's sad. My desire is to restore the Shankill Road back again to what it was, to restore the community spirit.

When I look back on it all, Ulster hasn't gained or lost one iota. The republicans haven't gained one iota. On the Falls Road, there's photos of loved ones on fireplaces that have been killed through the troubles and on the Shankill it's the same. The two families are shedding the same tears. It's not green tears or orange tears. They hurt the same. The same blood comes out of them. They're crying the same tears and that's what I try to tell the kids and the youth now, that paramilitaries can take you to two places – Roselawn Cemetery or Long Kesh, nowhere else. They leave people with a lot of heartache and grief.

George

Lucky Escape

It began as a normal evening trip into town. I left Beechmount Parade and flagged down a black taxi at the corner of Beechmount Avenue and Falls Road. As I sat down in the door side seat of the empty back, I saw that the driver and his companion in the front were both dressed in black gear and were not to be described as small men. I thought it a bit of a risk on their part to shoot the traffic lights at Broadway at high speed. Beyond the light, they increased speed, doing well over fifty mph along the Children's Hospital area. This was odd, and I began to think things were not right. I became sure of it as the driver overtook and passed two private cars at the main gate of St. Dominic's Girls' School. I began to believe I was in a serious position, and I was going cold and shivery, but I had a very heightened sense of my surroundings. I knew something was wrong now. This was NOT the normal Falls Road black taxi ride. What was it?

Suddenly I had a suspicion that I knew. As the taxi raced through the lights at the Royal Victoria junction, I sat well forward, both hands on the

door bar and opening handle. I tried to estimate how I could open the door and throw myself out, accepting some serious injury, but with a hope of staying alive in hospital. I now knew I was in the kind of taxi that the Falls Road people had been warned about. It was being driven by either UDA or UVF men, and I was in danger of being the next Catholic victim of a series of deaths caused by being trapped in a black taxi.

I next began to watch the road very carefully to pick my spot to jump. I did not have to do so. As we raced up to the Clonard Street/Falls Road junction, a private car shot out in front of us and our taxi braked suddenly to avoid a crash. I had all I needed. As the braking shot me forward I jerked the door open and hit the street running, almost fell twice and collapsed on the steps of the Hibernian Hall. The taxi I had left disappeared down the Falls at about seventy mph, and I lit a fag and sat until my pulse and nerves settled. I was very lucky to be alive.

To this day I don't recall what I did with the rest of the night.

Joe

The difficulty was, everybody had been conditioned to believe…

that if the Catholics got control, there could be rule from Rome and this 'bogeyman' was the religion thing. But the point is, we all grew up in the same circumstances, in terms of 'two-up, two-down', outside toilets, the worst of conditions. We in the Shankill weren't any better off than people in the Falls. But still, at election time, we had these people come round in suits and shirts and ties and they told us why we needed to vote for them. And when we recollected, they never told us to vote for them because they were going to get us better houses. They came round and they told us the reason we needed to vote for them was that we needed to keep Catholics out of jobs, because if they had our jobs, they would take control. Those were the things that were levelled at us, or told to us. I think in many ways working-class Prods believed they were better off than Catholics, and even though it was only slightly, they still believed they were better off. I think that's the card that the Ulster Unionists played at that time, and it was very successful. We grew up in that whole thing, and the whole notion about the siege of Derry, and the relief of Derry, and the Battle of the Boyne.

All of these things were told to us from when we were very, very young, and I suppose in many ways, this is what we grew up with, along with other things. They were all told in the context of – I'm not sure if I can describe it – told in terms of how people actually fought for what they believed in – for religious liberty and freedom and democracy. When I was growing up, most of the emphasis was put on the British Empire and British soldiers returning from Aden and Cyprus and all the other places there were wars. Stories of the soldiers coming home and finding it hard to get good houses and thinking they weren't getting very good treatment after having fought a war for democracy, and finding out that when they eventually were able to afford televisions and turn them on, the Germans and Japs were doing quite well, and they were doing very badly.

All that was the sort of stuff that was fed into us. Orangeism and the Battle of the Boyne were things that were there also and they were celebrated at a certain time of the year, but the whole year round, it was about the sacrifice that was made by Northern Irish people in terms of the Somme and the Second World War. That's what we were growing up on. It wasn't about hatred, because people spoke about Dubliners and Cork people who all fought alongside them in the British Army. All these things were talked of as a fight against something, depending on the period – religious freedom, fascism. All these things were portrayed in that way and in a very, very militaristic way rather than a political way. I think that's why, over the years, we've had bands. Marching bands, and blood and thunder bands. They've grown up out of that culture, a militaristic culture.

Billy

My brother and I got interested in First Aid from stories my father used to tell...

He was a first-aider in the local Inglis Bakery. With the heat, the ovens, the machinery and the chemicals, people were getting injured there on a daily basis.

Most of my family, and my wife's, are now involved with the medical side of things. I joined the British Red Cross as a cadet and went on to become an ambulance driver. I met my wife in 1977 in the Mater Hospital where she was training as a nurse. Over the years we've both come across people who have been injured or killed by the troubles. I mean, I know seven boys from my class in school who are all dead because of the violence. It's either at your front door, or it's across the street.

When I was working in the ambulance service some time around 1979 or 1980, we got a call to the Laganbank Road. There had been a shooting. A lone gunman had cycled across the Albert Bridge, shot his victim and got away. I happened to be on the Newtownards Road, and we raced to the scene. When we arrived, there was a crowd of people, and it turned out that the crowd had flagged down a car in the middle of the street, pulled the driver out, put the injured man in the back of the car and rushed him to hospital. I later discovered I'd gone to school with this fellow, so in a way, I'm glad not to have seen what he was like. He was basically shot dead at the scene.

It can be difficult, when you get a 999 call and when you arrive at the scene, maybe you know the person; maybe it's a sectarian murder; maybe it's a major incident; maybe you're having to deal with someone who's been the perpetrator. You don't think about it then. You're so highly trained, the split-second you arrive at the scene, there's certain procedures you have to implement. How many casualties are there? What types of injury? You have to put the hospital on stand-by. But the overriding thing is, you're there to save life, no matter whose life that is – even if it is the gunman or the bomber. You don't think of these things at the time. It's a human being, and they're injured and I've got to save their life. It's only later, listening to the news that you find out. That's the way it happened with the Shankill bomb.

In the Shankill bomb, one of the bombers was basically one of the first ones to be lifted, because he was outside the building. And nobody, but nobody, knew who he was. He was an injured person, and he was treated accordingly and taken to hospital. That day, it was a case of getting the injured into ambulances and taken to hospital, getting them away from the scene, and getting back again for the next serious injured and taking them away and then going back. As the day went on, obviously because of the devastation of the building, people were literally there with their hands, lifting brick and pieces of wood. Some of their injuries were horrific, absolutely horrific. And for every person who's lost their life, there's maybe twenty, thirty, forty people at the scene, screaming, because they know him, know her. Maybe it's a child. They're literally pulling at each other, trying to get in. They want to try and do something, but other people who are standing in the background are trying to keep them back, to let the nurses and the ambulance staff, the fire brigade, whoever, in. My overriding job is to get in, get people out, get them treated and get them to hospital.

After you've been out dealing with a major incident, like the Shankill bomb with multiple casualties and deaths, and all the casualties have been brought in, you go back to the hospital. It maybe takes you an hour to clean the vehicle, to wipe down everything, to wash it out and sterilise everything – change blankets, pillows, equipment. And you're covered. You get washed and you're shaking at this stage, because all the families are there and they're screaming. You're thinking of somebody you brought in alive but very seriously injured. The doctor comes out and calls the relatives in, and they walk out and they're screaming. So you know that person's been lost, and they're standing outside the casualty screaming. Cars arrive and people jump out – 'What's happened?' You're hearing all this. This is all going into your brain and you're seeing this. This is going through your eyes. In a case like a bomb, you can smell it and taste it – human flesh and hair. It's not nice... it's not nice.

At the time these things are happening, because of what you're doing, you don't think about them then, even though you know they're affecting you. It could be the next night, that night, sleepless nights or months later, years later that it hits you. Because of your training, because you've been on the job a long time, people think you can deal with it. Little do people realise that we're human beings as well. We're men in uniform. We're women in uniform. We're human beings as well. We suffer and feel the same as the person beside us who's watching this going on. The only difference is, we're actually dealing with it and taking it with us.

Laurence

When I arrived at the H-Blocks in 1978...

the Dirty Protest had already started and I, with a lot of others, declared ourselves political prisoners, thereby refusing to accept the British government's policy of criminalisation. As a result of our refusal to conform to the then existing prison rules, we had none of the privileges of the ordinary conforming prisoners. We didn't have access to our own clothes. We didn't have access to the radio, the television, newspapers or magazines. We were confined all day, every day to a small cell. We were cold. We did have blankets – we had three blankets, a chamber pot and a Bible.

By the time I had joined this particular protest, it had become known as 'The Dirty Protest', but I and my republican comrades, then and now, refer to it as 'The Blanket Protest'. We were known as the 'Blanket Men'.

The point of the protest was to object to and challenge the assault on our political convictions and our self-esteem, caused by the British government's failure to accept that what we were engaged in was a perfectly valid political struggle, albeit using physical force. That we didn't deny. I don't use the word violence. I'll use the word 'violence' if it's used comprehensively for everything from the United Nations to the British government, from the United States government, to the IRA, but not exclusively for republicans.

From our point of view, when we used force, it was first for defence, and then in the form of an offensive capacity when it was to establish a political goal which had been denied. Our beliefs. And as a result of that, when our self-esteem was challenged by the denial of political status. There were also a number of small factors, if you like, small insults that came to us as a result of that denial of self-esteem. For

example, at one stage, prisoners were expected to stand to attention outside the cell door, while the prison officers would do a head count. Nowadays, in most prisons, that would be accepted as totally unnecessary. It was an attempt to humiliate us through a regimentation of the prison population. Prison officers could have looked through cell doors to see if we were there or not, rather than militarily having us stand to attention outside our doors. The loss of self-esteem was a very, very personal feeling, for me and my friends and comrades, but we also had a very clear understanding that there were political stakes involved that bolstered us. We were bolstered by the politics of the situation.

I saw myself very much as an activist and participant in bringing about events. I was attempting to move a situation forward. Things didn't always come about as I wanted. They didn't always come about as I planned, but when someone has that part in a greater movement, I think they tend to ask themselves, 'What can I do to move things in the direction that I want them to move?' There's always a certain tension being an activist – can I make this commitment? I mean, I was on the Dirty Protest for over two years. I was on hunger strike for 53 days and I don't think I realised just how ill I was at that time, or how hard it was for my family. It took me a long time to realise this. There's always a conflict between the participation, and the agony and pain for the family and those around you. I've lost three brothers. My mother has buried three sons. I have lost a big part of my life to the prison system as a result of being an activist in a political struggle.

I don't look at these things from the point of view of a moral theologian, or a philosopher. I don't make those kind of moral judgments. I'm not saying I haven't any feelings. I do. But I see myself as a participant in a great movement of the time. I remember I once heard it put, to allow the cause to carry the responsibility and not the individual to carry the responsibility. In that sense, some may argue, that's to abdicate responsibility. But I see it as participating in a

Dublin make a very effective presentation at a meeting I was invited to. He outlined that a huge percentage of prisoners in his jail came from inner city areas of Dublin. These were the most deprived areas where unemployment and school drop-out rates were incredibly high, where housing conditions were very poor and where the sale,

movement that was a broad movement. It was a historical period in time. It was a period in history, and I participated in it so far as I know best, or as I saw best. I never sought the person behind the rifle and I have never seen the deaths of my three brothers as an individual's responsibility. If I blame anything, it's the state, the circumstances, not the individuals. If I have a cause, it's to change, or do away with, or transfer the state, which in this case we're talking about is the political state and the circumstances which brought this conflict about. I don't individualise or personalise the responsibility for it, as such. I'm afraid of introducing personalities into politics. To a certain extent people make up society and we can't move beyond the personality altogether, but I think if we start to look for individual responsibility, to blame Margaret Thatcher for the hunger strikes, to blame Ted Heath for internment, that's to distort the historical process.

I remember, about a year or eighteen months ago, listening to the prison governor in charge of Mountjoy Jail in

purchase and use of heroin and other drugs was common. He said, "How can we say that it's an individual being nasty?"

My attitude is, we've had a conflict, a civil conflict, and no one person or even ten persons were responsible on their own for that conflict. It's very rich to circle a small number of people and say, 'Ah, yeah yeah. There they are. Those boys up at Long Kesh there in the H-blocks, they're the perpetrators.' A lot of people that went through prison were actually victims perhaps before they were ever prisoners. In some ways, it's even more frightening to think that the conflict was not the result of a handful of evil men. We all together managed, or mis-managed a situation. Essentially, we weren't able to agree on how the place was best governed. As a result of that, we had an irreconcilable conflict over government. We had a civil war.

Tommy

My Worst Nightmare

The yard was warm after a blistering day in early August. My husband and I were washing the leatherette pram body with the help of our two young children who played companionably with water and sponges. That warm summer evening I can truly say I was content. A time I would like to have put a cog in the axis of the world, to hold it still, just for a little while. We cleaned the chrome and layered it with Vaseline to keep it from rusting.

My husband's aunt appeared in the gateway of the yard and surveyed our work, asking what we were at. "Oh," I quipped, teasing her, "We're cleaning up the pram here for Shae" and waited for her usual comment, "Two will do you, one for each hand." I was referring to a son we would have some time in the future. We already had two little girls, and thought Mandy, one year old, would have been a boy so the name was left aside again. I can't remember if we actually put the pram in the loft that night.

The scene is etched in my mind as the last normal thing we did together for a long time.

I saw the political scene at this time in 1971 as interesting, not really threatening. Just interesting. And we had heard the word and term 'internment' bantered about a lot. Coming from a Protestant background, I thought little about it and knew even less.

On that warm August evening I had no idea what horror the future held for this island, or how many would die. No idea how long it would continue and that my son, that I did not even know was conceived, would know nothing else but 'the troubles' as he grew up.

We lived in a terrace of six houses with a lane-way along the back between our yards and the garden. That night I had a dream. I dreamt that the entire terrace was surrounded by soldiers standing to attention, approximately twenty feet apart, with guns at the ready – like sentry guards. I also saw army trucks parked near by. This was the total substance of the dream. Nothing else happened. Just the soldiers' threatening presence.

I looked at the clock. It was 4.15 am and I dismissed it as nothing more than the influence of the increasing army presence in the town. However, I was to rethink my views on this dramatically when on 9th August 1971, a few days later, our front door was smashed in at 4.15 am and my husband was dragged away to waiting trucks. I remember leaping from bed, looking out the window, watching and in the grey light before dawn, I saw the soldiers from my dream, standing twenty feet apart, like sentries, guns held at the ready.

The noise had awoken the children and so I took them

both into my bed and tried to stay calm. I had no telephone and could not contact anyone at this time of the morning. It was my husband's 27th birthday and his presents were piled by the breakfast bench for him to open before going to work.

I asked my next-door neighbour to keep an eye on the kids and at 9.00 am sharp I stood in a telephone box phoning my solicitor, Jack McCann. He broke the news to me. "It's here," he said. "This is internment."

The phone fell from my shaking hand and I sobbed deeply, feeling the world spin around me. His voice talking in the distance from the phone, which swung rhythmically from its cord brought me back. I took hold of it and placed it to my ear. I apologised and asked him to tell me again.

No one had any idea where the people lifted were. All had been lifted at 4.15 a.m. that morning in dawn swoops all over the North. Talk was of Magilligan, perhaps Long Kesh, new prison camps just whispered about. Or they could be in Bally-kelly, an existing RAF base, as we were on the Derry side. He would try to find out and keep in touch.

Days passed. I don't remember what I told the children. I was 21 years old with two young children – on my own – in a politically explosive and dangerous situation. Once word got out that my husband was a suspected terrorist, there was no telling what might happen in this small loyalist town. I was terrified. But this did not show as I went about like a zombie, head held high doing my usual daily tasks. On the outside, I was coping remarkably. Inside, I was falling apart.

My memory of the troubles was that they did not really become dangerous until after the introduction of intern-ment. This is when I think it really began.

I refused to have anyone stay with me at night, wanting my own space to grieve. I cannot recall all the emotions I felt then. I know, without losing my husband to death, he felt completely lost and I grieved as if he was dead. The isolation and the sudden tearing of us apart. The things that were his in the bathroom, the socks, items of clothing, books, silly notes we wrote to each other tore me apart day and night. I slept badly and was beginning to be sick each morning. On top of everything else – I was pregnant again.

I seldom cried as I was terrified I'd never stop if I started. And I could not frighten the girls. So we sang, we walked, we told stories and life went on somehow. I remember looking in the mirror and wondering how I could possibly look so normal when inside I felt so different. Not at all the same person.

About ten days later, my husband was located aboard the prison ship *Maidstone* in Belfast Lough. I believe he was the first prisoner to receive a visit and I the first visitor. Ingeniously arranged by Jack McCann, who I always believed could work miracles. I remember walking along the quayside and seeing the men's faces pressed to the portholes, watching me. Being shown into a Portakabin with a chair and a border with mesh wire two feet apart, a plastic grid and more mesh wire. My husband was shown in. He was barely recognisable. Thin and gaunt with several days growth. It took every semblance of sanity I possessed to smile and say the most ridiculous, "How are you?"

It was here, in this hideous place, I told him I thought we had conceived our son. The haunted eyes filled with tears and I knew he wanted to hold me. But we could not touch. So we just stared hard into each other's eyes in silence. I didn't cry then but I cry as I write, seeing the scene before me now in replay. I couldn't cry then. I had to hold on somehow. To cry was weak, it was to give in. It was about straight shoulders and insolent glances at my husband's jailers. I walked away, leaving him staring after me.

Life fell into a pattern of letters and visits after that. No benefit. No categorisation for internees. In fact, I received several letters, which I still have, from the DHSS which informed me they regretted that I was not entitled to benefit as my husband could adequately provide for me.

He was a non-person. He was not with me and he was not, technically, a prisoner.

As things hotted up on the political scene, it emerged that the government were breaking the law holding people indefinitely and so a hasty change in the law was introduced. Trumped-up charges were called upon to substantiate holding the internees longer – in my husband's case, eight months longer. The day our son was born, he was in court on a charge of possessing illegal literature – a *United Irishman* newspaper. I spent the day in court and went across the road to the maternity home to have our child alone.

My husband received a three-month sentence and was taken to Crumlin Road Prison. It was here, six weeks later, he met his son for the first time. While I was frightened and intimidated by the clanging of the metal doors of the prison, my husband assured me that the conditions here were much better than in Long Kesh.

The fact that he was now a sentenced prisoner changed the situation a little. It removed the uncertainty. We had a release date, three months down the line. But when it arrived, he was rearrested outside Crumlin Road Prison and taken back to Long Kesh. And so we began again.

Christmas came and went. I wrote to my husband all day long, recapturing everything that was happening. The children's reaction to their presents, how they had posed out in the front garden in their red and white Christmas outfits as people passing to Mass admired them.

In September, he was released without warning or explanation. We later filed for and won compensation for unlawful imprisonment.

Heather

S i d e m o u t h   **L e s s o n**

"You're looking for trouble
if you open your mouth fully
in this town – Jesus! –
shouting about Derry and the RUC.

Sidemouth. Learn to sidemouth.
Pass the words out of the side
of your mouth, across your face,
over the table,
and slowly
and quietly
show them to me.

This is the Big Belfast Poker Game,
you're not in Derry now.
Cover them cards.
Watch the other tables.
Sidemouth, for fuck sake. Sidemouth!"

Joe

Four Bombs

The second bomb was planted in a beautiful pub on the shores of Lough Neagh. It used to be a coaching inn, where the teams of horses were changed on the stagecoaches travelling between Belfast and Derry in the old days. There were three rooms in the place – two bars and a small room where musicians usually gathered. That night all of them were crowded. We went into the larger bar, met some friends and managed to find a couple of seats. We were there only about five minutes when the door burst open and a woman appeared. She shouted frantically above the chatter, "Look out, look out, there's a bomb in the hall!"

I looked past her and there it was – a squat object sitting on the floor with a detonator sparking on the top of it. There was immediate panic. Everyone jumped up to run, but there was nowhere to run to. There was no way out except past the bomb.

We ended up all piled up beneath, behind and around the bar counter, which was as far as we could get from the door leading to the hall. I crouched on my hands and knees on the floor waiting in terror for the explosion – but nothing happened.

This was no thanks to the bombers but was due entirely to the bravery of the owner's son. The owner had been sitting in the hallway keeping guard, as many pubs were being targeted at that time by loyalists. The fact that he was a Catholic would have been enough for them, though the pub's clientele was mixed. He was sitting there when a man walked in carrying the bomb. He set it on the floor without a word and walked out again, got into a car and was driven away. The owner had the presence of mind to run out after him and get the car number. However, it was his son who rushed over to the bomb and pulled out the smoking detonator, with only a few inches to go before it reached the explosive. I know this because he showed it to me later.

Jill

A Hero & a Loved One

I never thought the troubles had come close to me and my family, but when I was nine, I discovered my family's tragic history and I would like to share it with you. I would like to tell you about my grandfather who was a policeman.

In August 1972, granddad was on duty at Waterloo Street when suddenly two bangs came out of nowhere. The bullets hit him in the lung and the thigh. Amazingly, he walked from Waterloo Street to the Strand Road Barracks before he collapsed. As the ambulance was speeding to the scene, grandad's condition was rapidly getting worse. When the ambulance eventually reached the barracks, he was immediately rushed to intensive care, which wasn't a good sign. His health was on and off for a few weeks and he didn't appear to get any better. Then grandad eventually started to improve and you could call that a miracle.

The bullets damaged his lung and thigh quite badly. He has to be very careful in the winter to prevent catching a cold or flu which then infects his lung. He has a slight limp during the cold weather and suffers from stiffness as a result of his injuries. From that horrific incident, I am proud to say he's still with us today. To me he's a hero and a loved one. I know my two brothers feel the same as I do.

Since finding out about the incident, I am now quite frightened of the thought of it happening again. I worry about my family and don't feel safe wherever we go. I remember always having to check under our car before we drove anywhere. Mum and Dad pretended they had to check the tyres each morning, but I knew we were looking under the car for something. There was a policeman living nearby who didn't check his car and his family got into it and drove off. There was a bomb attached, but fortunately the bomb dropped off the car without going off. They were saved, but had to move away immediately. All of this story is true and really did happen to my family.

Another thing that makes me sad is that I can't say names for safety reasons. I would like to read my story to my friends, but I know I cannot because a lot of my classmates don't approve of the RUC. My dad is also in the RUC and my friends often ask me what he works as. I have to make something up to hide his identity and I am frightened of being bullied or picked on because I am an RUC man's son.

After the Good Friday Agreement, I think it is reasonable that adults should talk about their differences without violence and killings of innocent people. I think adults are being unreasonable when they will not talk about peace and their differences without using guns and threats.

Mark, aged 12

When they made my daddy

because I don't think I've ever known anyone like him in all my life. I don't know how he managed it, but for a long time, he kept us sheltered from the troubles. As a child, I was aware there was something going on. Sometimes we'd have been rushed to my granny's house, off the Shankill, if there was trouble in Ardoyne. When we came back to the house, there would sometimes be mattresses up against the windows, but we were mostly pampered from the stone-throwing and the petrol bombs on the street.

It was 1969 when it finally erupted and people had started moving out of the Protestant end of the street, leaving empty houses. I remember a large meeting in the church hall, and a decision came from that to move out all together, because the Protestant people were being closed in. I remember things like lorries getting brought into the streets and people rushing their things out. When this started happening, the people at the bottom end of the street – the Catholic people (I'm not talking about all the Catholic people. I'm talking about the ones that had been out stone-throwing) – were aware that we had started to move out, and they came from the bottom end of the street, torching the houses as they came up. We were the very top house of the street. My father put us onto the lorry along with what possessions we could get out of the house in time. And he went back in again and threw petrol under the stairs, and put a light to it and said no Fenian would move into his house. We were crying in the lorry because we knew we weren't going back again to the house. But it must have been ten times worse for him because he lived all his life in that house except when he got married and moved out for a few years. It must have been really hard for him. People were busying about and getting their own wee bits and pieces onto lorries. A fellow we knew actually got his leg amputated that day. Things like that

they threw the mould away…

stick in my head from when we actually moved. We moved into a large block of maisonettes at the top of Ballysillan Park that had just been put up. Everybody that moved into those maisonettes were squatting, because they'd nowhere else to go.

My father was an engineer. My mother was a book binder in a printers and they worked hard all their life to build a home for us. It was hard bringing six of a family into a relatively new house and building it up from scratch again. But they did it. They did it within a couple of years. You would never have knew it was a new home just started.

He never talked much about it all after we did move. He probably did to my mummy, but we would never have heard him discussing how he felt about it. But you knew, because he was a lot quieter after he moved. In 1987, he had a heart attack, so he took early retirement and got something like £16,000. To tell you the truth, the two of them never had such money all their life. It didn't come through until the June of 1988 and they decided, 'Right, we'll go away to Donegal for a weekend together.' There was a wee place called The Downings in Donegal, where they took us every year on a camping holiday. But they wanted to go on their own, so they went in June. But before they went, my mummy had mentioned about a lump on her head. When they came back, she wasn't feeling very well and they felt this lump and it had got really, really big over the weekend. They took her to the hospital and done tests, and told her she had lung cancer. They told her she maybe had six or eight weeks to live. And that was it. She went downhill really quick after that. Out of the £16,000 my mummy got a leather coat and a pair of boots before she died and my daddy never got over the death of her. But the very fact they got that holiday together before she died was something, I suppose.

After my mummy died, we all rounded up on daddy for support, and we would have started talking about things like Ardoyne on an odd night if we had all got together. He would have talked about it then, about how much he blamed the people there for making him move, the Catholics in Ardoyne, for this at the time. He said it was years before he could get over that feeling.

It must have been really hard for all the men moving out with their families and having to start making a home again for them. But I know my daddy – he was a man I always looked up to and respected. I mean, I always appreciated my father, and my mother, for trying to cushion us from the problems there was in Ardoyne. It wasn't until the actual move really, or the odd stone thrown, that we knew there was anything wrong, and I'm sure it was going on long before that. But they kept that away from us, which must have been really hard for them to do.

Pheme

My parents are originally from Hong Kong New Territories...

which is where the majority of Chinese people in Northern Ireland are from. They came over to Northern Ireland back in the 1960s which is when Chinese people first started to arrive here. Most of the people from the New Territories would have lacked a formal education, but my father did have an education. He trained as a teacher and taught geography for a while. His English was better than average, but he didn't have the confidence to pursue a teaching profession here – so like a lot of Chinese people, he set up his own business in catering.

My mum and dad had one daughter when they came over, but she was left in the New Territories with my grandmother and didn't come over to Northern Ireland until the 70s. The rest of us were born in Northern Ireland – my four sisters, my brother and myself. I am the youngest member of the family. Most of us were born in Larne, and when I was born, we moved to Glengormley which is where the family home still is.

Both my parents worked very solidly, so they got other people to mind us a lot. Most of my siblings were looked after by a lady from Larne. By the time I was born, my mum's Chinese cousin had settled in Northern Ireland. He was married to an English woman who had five children of her own, and so she began to take care of me; so I was brought up by an English aunt who I consider as my mum, so I've sort of got two mums. I was six years old when I eventually went home to live with my real family, and it was all a bit of a culture clash, because I felt I didn't really know them well.

I attended the school nearest to my home which happened to be Catholic, so we all grew up with a Catholic education. The lady from Larne was actually a Protestant, whereas my auntie was a Catholic which meant that unlike my brother and sisters, I was brought up in Catholic traditions. I was made to go to Mass and do all the Catholic things, whereas my brother and sisters, while they had the Catholic education, weren't sent to Mass or made to do the other traditional Catholic things. My real parents didn't mind either way. Having said that, I can remember my father coming to an open night in school once and talking to the priest who taught RE and saying to him, "I don't want you teaching my son religion. I don't want him to become a priest." I remember him saying something like that and very much stomping his ground as if to say, 'OK, you're here to teach him academically. Don't be teaching him any of this religion stuff.' I'm the only one of the children, apart from another sister in Liverpool, who has been baptised and confirmed, and that helped me, gave me a stronger identity. In the religious sense, my identity wasn't confused at all, as it was in other areas of my life where I always felt slightly on the outside.

Being able to speak good English also helped me to fit in. There were individual incidents where people would call me names because I was Chinese, but usually, as soon as I opened my mouth, people accepted me as one of them. Having said that, I was, on one occasion, beaten up outside school while I was waiting for a bus. My attackers made it known to me that I was being singled out for being a 'chinky' and for being a 'Fenian'. There are so few Chinese people, you can get into trouble for being different, but being different can also be to your advantage. You can feel unique, like a big fish in a small pond, whereas if you were across the water in the States or whatever, you'd be one of many children from other cultures.

It's difficult to remain objective in Northern Ireland. Chinese people would like to think that the troubles have nothing to do with them, but inevitably, living in such a sectarian city, where all the housing estates are divided by religion, you begin to assume the beliefs of whatever community you happen to be in. A lot of people just find themselves going along with one side or the other, just to fit in. Sometimes it isn't a case of sympathy but of necessity. It's not always an option. I mean, with myself, I wouldn't describe myself as a republican, but I've an outlook on life that's more Catholic, and that affects my attitude to the troubles, which is not unbiased. As far as the Chinese community are concerned, this is not something you choose. You don't pick an area to live in because it's Catholic or Protestant, but because there's an opportunity for a business and that's it. In the case of my auntie, that was difficult. She was a Catholic living in an area that was predominantly Protestant. Before the troubles started, people knew that she was a Catholic and didn't have a problem with it. As the troubles heightened, this changed, and she and the children started to get harassed. There would be things written on the wall like 'Taigs Out' but there would also be 'Chinky' things written as well, even though her children were only half Chinese. I was sitting by the window one day, and a brick came through it. My head was showered with glass. To me, this is the perfect example of how racism and sectarianism are interlinked in Northern Ireland. That's where it all gets mixed up. Is it sectarianism or is it racism? I think the same people who are likely to be sectarian are the ones who would be racist as well. It doesn't take a big leap of imagination to suggest that a bigot will discriminate and perpetrate on a whole range of issues.

There's a term among the Chinese community which is quite racist in itself – 'banana' – yellow on the outside, white on the inside. Being a 'banana' myself and growing up in Northern Ireland, which is my home, the troubles completely spoil the place where I live. It's a beautiful country, a potentially great place to be. The troubles affect me, because of what happened to my auntie and how she was driven out. She left for England when I was 13 or 14, and that's a fairly crucial stage of one's life in a way, growing up and all that. Because of it, I was forced to grow up without a mother, because that's what she was to me. I do blame the troubles for that. To end on a positive note, however, my experiences of life growing up in Northern Ireland have instilled in me a desire to work towards the betterment of this society in terms of enabling people to view the difference and diversity that exists here as something which is to be embraced, not frowned upon.

Chun Kiu

My First Memories of The Troubles

The first memories of the troubles I have are when three men were shot dead at the entrance to the estate where I live. I am not quite sure of the year. It was the early 80s and I was about seven. It was quite late on when the incident happened. I was in bed and just about to fall asleep when I heard what I thought were thousands of shots ringing out and I knew it wasn't too far away. Although the shots only lasted a few seconds, to me it seemed as though they would never stop, and I was petrified. I couldn't move, and neither my sister or I made a single move in case the 'bad men' came to get us in our beds.

As I stared into the darkness, I felt alone and scared, wanting my mother but afraid to go and look for her. I felt sick, and got the same ominous feeling in the pit of my stomach that I always get when something bad happens. I thought that the bogeyman was real and was lurking in the bushes waiting to shoot someone, and it might be me the next time.

My memories seem so innocent because I did not understand what had happened or why. I was soon educated by never-ending news bulletins showing over and over again the disturbing scene of the pale blue car riddled with bullet holes and the tape that cordoned off the area. It was my area. Here I played with my friends, rode my bike, and started off on walks with my family.

Now my area was at the centre of a triple murder investigation. As I looked on, I thought I would never go out again. How could the place where I live be like this and what would be next? Some of the questions being asked were, 'Who were the victims?', 'Where did they live?', 'Were they married?', and 'Why were they killed?' I could not fully feel secure and often felt anxious and worried that

somebody might break into our house and hurt my family the way others have been violated.

From then on I regarded any news broadcasts as depressing and saddening. Practically every night there was a report of someone being shot, blown up or maimed. The news made me feel frustrated, sad, trapped and in a way completely helpless. I wanted to do something, to say something, but what good would it do? It seemed to me that there were people who talked with bullets and not words, and I couldn't communicate with them because I wasn't prepared to speak that language.

I hated watching the news, but at the same time felt compelled to, as if it were better to know what was going on. I felt like a passenger on a ship wanting to know if the storm was getting any closer. Not that I could do anything if it was, but take cover and go somewhere safe until it settled. For a while at least.

Julie-Ann

Grandfather James Stewart had three weaknesses…

drink, politics and cricket. He had a fine library in his small kitchen house. His collection had a strong Irish influence with the emphasis on social history. He was a Protestant nationalist, supported Home Rule and was very vociferous in his opposition to the Great War. Frequently, when he had a few drinks, he expressed his views in public and was doing so when the black-edged telegram arrived at my great-grandfather Hamilton's house informing him of the death of his son, James, at the Somme. My grandfather was always very conscious of his family's support for 'the turn-out' and proud of the part they played in the time of 'the hurry'. His opinions greatly influenced my father. They both supported the 1916 Rising in Dublin. As soon as he came of age, he joined the IRA on the Shankill Road. He fought in the War of Independence, eventually siding with De Valera in the civil war.

During the treaty negotiations in 1920–1921, the attacks on isolated Catholic families and small Catholic enclaves intensified. Great pressure was exerted on Collins to do something practical to alleviate the distress. An unofficial force of sixty officers and men was set up with the emphasis placed on defence and strict orders not to take offensive action under any circumstances. My father was ordered to the Marrow Bone.

My mother's father and his two brothers served with the British Army on the Western Front. It's ironic that my Catholic grandfather supported the Great War and served in the British Army while my Protestant grandfather opposed the war and was not prepared to serve either King or Kaiser. My Catholic grandfather, however, after the war joined Sinn Féin and it was from his house the picket set out to take up their defensive positions in the Marrow Bone. His house was a sort of base for operations and it was there my father met my mother. Of course, she was very young – only a child. She was born in 1908.

After the signing of the treaty my father supported de Valera's opposition to the Free State. He joined a flying column in east Mayo/west Roscommon. Their objective was to stop the advance of the Free State army up the west coast. With the death of General Liam Lynch, most of the opposition to the Free State collapsed. They were ordered to ditch arms and return home. My father eventually made his way back to Belfast and there was captured. In Crumlin Road jail he was given the opportunity to sign the paper. That meant signing away his political beliefs in return for his freedom. He refused and was imprisoned on the prison ship *Argenta*, laying anchor in Larne Lough. With the disappearance of the republican threat, he was eventually released and came back to Belfast.

During the 30s, he joined the Irish Communist Party and was very active in the Outdoor Relief Strikes. During the war years Catholics had difficulty getting employment. Most of the men in the Marrow Bone worked in the building industry. A couple worked in the Post Office, some as tram conductors and a number were red-leaders in the shipyard. Few, if any, were in the skilled trades. Housing and jobs were the two scarce commodities in the Marrow Bone. They were used as political weapons. Often priests were offered jobs for their parishioners by Corporation officials in return for votes. Housing was used in the same way. Often prospective tenants had to pay key money. An added insult to the community was a whore-house on the Oldpark Road where the City Fathers left keys of houses and folk had to face the added humiliation of going and almost begging this madame for a key, even though they were paying for it.

Eventually to get work my father had to go to England. He was working in Cadbury's chocolate factory. He used to send us parcels of Whole Nut: big lumps of twisted, nut-filled chocolate. We looked forward to that monthly delivery; it was our treat. That pleasure only lasted a few months. His file was sent to the English police by the RUC. He was arrested and deported back to Belfast. We didn't let it get us down. My father had a great knack for seeing humour in most incidents, however delicate. He described in great detail his arrest and the reaction of his landlady. He acted the whole scene as we sat around the fire. It was hilarious. My childhood was very happy and pleasant. My mother had the greatest admiration for my father and she instilled in us children the same admiration. We were in awe of him – he was God to us.

My father's employment prospects weren't enhanced by his political record. He would have worked at anything. Once he got a job in a market garden. When my mother questioned his knowledge of gardening he answered, "Sure isn't the library full of gardening books." I was dispatched to the Oldpark Library. When the librarian questioned my father's interest in gardening, in view of the fact that he didn't have a garden, I was very annoyed. This mere librarian scoffing at my father, "My father's getting a plot on the Westland Road," I snapped as I gathered the books from the counter.

The names of the flowers were in Latin and he was annoyed when we couldn't read them for him. He thought because we went to Mass on Sunday, we knew Latin. "I might as well have sent you all to the Ebenezer Gospel Hall. I heard more Latin on the Shankill Road." To please him, we made up names. 'Dominus Vobiscum' became 'Dom-in-I-us Vob-is-cure-him'. He got the job and tied labels with these names on a number of plants. He was soon caught on and got the sack. As we sat around the fire he acted out the words of his employer and his subsequent dismissal. "There are plants all over the Malone Road with names unheard of in the gardening world!"

The pressures of getting work and supporting a growing family pushed politics into the back seat. He became disillusioned with de Valera and the Fianna Fáil party. Slowly his interests waned, but never completely disappeared.

James

Before the Whole World Dies

Hello, my name is Aisling. I am 11 years old and have not experienced many troubles. But last year, in 1998, I was up the town with my mum and my sister and I experienced something I would not like to experience again. It was that four masked men hijacked a bus. There was an elderly lady on the bus. One of the men grabbed her and threw her down three steps of the bus and drove away. I also was walking with my mum, my dad, my brother and my sister at the Bogside when a bus got hijacked and was burned out.

On Bloody Sunday my mum's cousin Bernard McGuigan was killed, and it was a terrible tragedy for her family. Bloody Sunday was a tragedy for all the people who had relatives injured or killed. Thirteen people were killed and they were Hugh Gilmour, Bernard McGuigan, Gerald McKinney, John Young, Patrick Doherty, William Nash, Jim Wray, Michael Kelly, Kevin McElhinney and Jack Duddy.

There was also a boy called Danny Devenney aged 13. He knelt and prayed at his father's graveside. There also was a seven year old planting a bomb by the rubbish tips. He also nearly got killed by a plastic bullet. There also was a 14 year old got first aid because of the injuries he had. Many people still die because of troubles still going on today and it is terrible all those people are dead.

I hope they will finish before the whole world dies.

Aisling, aged 11

The following is the complete list of those who lost their lives on Bloody Sunday: Patrick 'Pat' Doherty, Gerald Donaghy, John 'Jack' Duddy, Hugh Gilmore, Michael Kelly, Michael McDaid, Kevin McElhinney, Bernard 'Barney' McGuigan, Gerald McKinney, William McKinney, William Nash, James Wray, John Young.

Fifteen Lines for Omagh

I shall not describe in pretty terms or metaphors
our making love that morning.
I shall not enumerate in rhyme or any verse
events occurring miles away.
I shall not mix children's faces in any palette,
tally-up a shopping list
or place a bet.
I shall not chide advice by any voice
nor poets' silences at times like these,
not even talk or write about the weather.
Romantic murder mocks
and robs the pen of power.
Today there are no terms or metaphors,
no lexicon can call a single syllable to mind.
I shall not describe.

Dennis

The End of My Immunity

I was there. Right at the moment of ignition. Right at the moment when this man-made piece of hell engulfed its victims. But I was at a safe distance. I was a witness. I am a guilty survivor and this is my account for what it is worth.

I was leaving back a video to Xtravision. I usually park in an alley beside the store. For the first time in ages, I couldn't find a parking space. The carnival, I supposed. After two or three minutes of useless manoeuvring, I decided to just drive back to the top of the alley. I left the car running and dashed into the video store. After returning to the car, I quickly took my place in the traffic lane facing Market Street. I was about five or six cars back from the lights and as I went to adjust the car stereo there was a crack.

My eyes were drawn to a momentary yellow and white flash. Dark shapes in the distance hurled from the flash like clay. Almost simultaneously hundreds of slates were launched straight up in the air like beads of sweat from a boxer's head. There was so much happening all at once, but it seemed normal for a second, maybe something to do with the carnival I thought, incredibly.

Those few stunned seconds of silence were overtaken by awful screaming, wailing and shouting. I looked up at the sun as it beat down unconcerned. Bombs don't go off on sunny days like this, I thought. Bombs! Oh fuck. This is a bomb. A big bomb! Reality hit me. It was getting hard to breathe. I had nervous tickles in my stomach.

The strangest things go through my mind at moments of crisis. The image of the slates kept flashing through my consciousness and all I could think of was those little snowstorm paperweights, but the snow was black slate, smoke and dust.

Just after the bomb had exploded, its blast came down towards my line of cars like a wind from hell, shaking my car ever so gently but mowing down pedestrians on both pavements. Glass, sucked from shop windows, shot back and forth across the street, its glint being caught in the burning sun like slivers of rain. I felt like someone in a submarine, protected by my car's metal and glass. I was safe in the quiet environment of my car, protecting me like a womb but letting me witness the unfolding mayhem.

I sat there, still stunned to a point, but now found myself getting out of the car. As I opened the door, the volume of the noise rocketed. My senses and sanity were swamped and overwhelmed now by women who seemed to be everywhere, bleeding and screaming, some moaning in strange chants as if transported back to infancy by shock and pain. I could see the bombsite now ahead in the near distance. The curtain of smoke almost lifted, revealing the stuff of nightmares. Debris, glass, rubble and bodies lay around.

I began to think maybe the few extra moments spent trying to park the car had prevented me from being at the head of the traffic lights, only yards from the bomb. I could see ahead of me the shrapnel-peppered car that was at the foot of the lights. That could have been me, I thought.

My heart seemed to be beating all over my body, in my ears, in my chest, in my stomach. Hypnotised into a trance-like state by the pure horror, I started to walk towards the scene. I tried to run but I couldn't. People were still screaming around me, wide-eyed, most marked and bloodied to some degree. Some were crying and some couldn't manage it, their mouths just open.

Then from the corner of my eye, I saw a man lying on the pavement, rolling about on his spine, his legs trying to reach the foetal position. He was losing blood from his arm and face. A few men stood around, bewildered, with him at their feet. All I could think of from a first aid course years ago, was to put him in the recovery position. I blurted out the suggestion. The men seemed relieved to hear the idea. We put him on his side. Then my useful suggestions dried up. I tried hard to think. Out of nowhere, a man arrived, introduced himself as a nurse and took control. His professionalism injected me with self-belief. He found the man's worst injury, which was his arm,

and showed me how to cup his elbow with my hand while keeping the arm tight to the body to stem the blood flow all the while explaining his actions to his patient. Then he was gone, his expertise needed elsewhere.

Things like this don't happen in Omagh.

I cup the man's elbow. Blood oozes down through my fingers, palm, and wrist. His blood is warm but the sun is warmer, drying it into my hands like paint. I concentrate on informing my patient that he isn't going to die. Again and again I tell him. He cannot tell me if he agrees as he has not spoken since I have been with him. I don't know this man or his beliefs. All I know about him is his suffering. Everything else is so irrelevant now.

Cops without their caps and clad in black boilersuits arrive. Cars and vans are being commandeered hastily, their owners now ambulance drivers. I shout to a passing cop that my man needs help. He scans his condition for a second and away he goes, arriving back in a van from a local business. The man is put into the van with efficiency if not great ceremony. Soon it is full of the walking-wounded and worse. The activity surrounding the van is in contrast with those lying within.

It struck me in my stomach… FIONA! My sister Fiona. She is usually in Omagh on a Saturday. My body weakened as I lurched towards the bombsite and the bodies. I was almost running now towards what was left of Market Street. Shops and buildings I knew well, almost unrecognisable now, indistinguishable from each other, no marks of identification remaining, just rubble in the foreground and sinister blackness behind what was left of the doorways and windows.

Then I saw the first pile of bodies. Nothing you have ever seen delivers the same feeling. I realised they were women, but I couldn't seem to see their faces or even their heads. Maybe I didn't let myself see. I don't know. I wanted to run far away, but knew there was no place far enough to hide from horror like this. It occurred to me that I would never forget these scenes or this horrible feeling.

I shook myself, but my head was spinning, my body limp. My mouth was dry. I pressed on up the street where two hundred or so had stood oblivious of the bomb parked among them. I now found myself looking for my sister. I was carrying out the worst task of my life and I was not alone. Other pale-faced people were doing the same.

I kept going up the hill, making promises to God, bargaining for my sister. My eyes were lifted from the ground by the noise of feet tramping on the rubble and short clipped instructions: "Steady!" "Watch that stone," "Come on, faster."

I was finding it very hard to hold it together – occasionally whimpering like a tired child, fighting back a desire to scream and roar. Another small group of corpses caught my eye. I turned to look, frightened to do so, my sister never far from the private nightmare of my mind while I carried out my inspections.

The water which I could now see was coming from what must have been the bomb crater, was trying to wash the corpses down the slight hill near the end of Market Street. 'Is there a God?' I questioned myself. 'Who lets this happen to the innocent?'

The dead seemed everywhere, in shops, on the street, good people lying destroyed before me, better people than me, I was sure.

I decided I could not go on trying to find my sister. Coming through the noise, I heard people shouting that the phone lines were down. Something told me that the public phones at the bus depot would be working, even though all the phones here were out. I figured they were on a different line from the bomb site. I headed down the street, hoping to hear that my sister was not in Omagh. It was my only consolation. Feeling useless among people who could not be helped, I went back down Market Street trying to ignore things that you can't. Police and fire-fighters were covering the dead at the bottom of the street with curtains, or whatever else was at hand. An Ulsterbus now parked in the junction box was filled with bloodied survivors.

I was sprinting now past cars, abandoned, with doors lying open like the scene of a nuclear aftermath. I never thought it would come to my door. I thought I had immunity. Newsreel pictures of Bloody Sunday and Enniskillen and all the news reports I had witnessed as a child of the troubles came back to haunt me now.

The enormity of it all was beginning to take hold. I was

conscious of my hands again, sticky and almost dry. I could see people along the road, their eyes fixed on my bloodied forearms as I pulled at the air to go faster. The depot came into view. The suspense was building now, choking me, putting pressure on my lungs. I could receive relief or the prospect of even more sickening suspense. I could feel myself getting older as I neared the phone boxes.

A small crowd had gathered around the phones. They all bombarded me with desperate questions: "Is there people hurt over there?" "Is there anybody dead?" "Where was the bomb?" It seemed as if in return for my information I could get using the phone. I blurted out my answers and I might as well have hit them. "There's at least ten or fifteen dead. It went off near the bottom of Market Street." Some of the women crumpled like paper bags.

Finally, I was in the phone box and, like the car, it cocooned me from the noise and the immediate reality. I slotted in the ten pence and punched in my parents' number, my hand shaking. For the first time I could hear my panting breath. The phone rang one… two… three times. My mother picked up. For a moment I could not speak. "Hello?" she said.

"Hello. Hello!" I blurted.

"Is that you, Stephen?"

"Aye. It's me. Jesus Christ, is Fiona there? There's been a massive bomb. Half of Omagh is gone. There's bodies everywhere. Jesus! Jesus! There must be fifteen or twenty."

"Hold on Stephen. Now calm down. Talk slowly."

"Is Fiona there?"

"No."

"WHAT?"

"But she's okay, she's with Brendan. It's okay. Oh. No. Wait a minute… They're here. She's just arrived outside the door in Brendan's car. They're both here. Wait, here she is."

"Hello? Stephen? I'm here. It's Fiona."

Tears flowed. At last I could cry. And cry I did, like a baby. My mother told me that my father would call up to my flat and to meet him there. I told everybody I loved them before I hung up.

As I neared the site on the way back to the car it drew me up towards its black heart once more, but the dead were covered now, giving them some dignity. As I walked once more over the debris and glass, I saw a man I recognised standing guard outside a shop, but he was not like a sentry on duty. He was dishevelled, his posture that of defeat, and his face racked in pain, and disbelief. His wife lay within – dead. A fireman was with him. I think he was trying to keep him out of the unsafe building for his own good. His own good! What would that poor man know about the word 'good' now?

I could see the courthouse and the remains of the car bomb in the near distance. I make my way home. I have not been hurt and I lost no-one, yet I cannot count my blessings.

I am cold and empty inside.

Stephen

I believe the way forward for this country...

is through people being integrated, be it in education or whatever. You need to put children together from the start, when they're very young and integration should involve a discussion on what we're about. It shouldn't be about 'We're all neutral'. It should be about 'I'm British', or 'I'm Irish', or 'I'm a cross between the two', or whatever it is. It should be about why you are who you are and why you're proud to be who you are, and why you're not a threat to someone else. It's about learning tolerance.

I learnt some of this through my son, who goes to an integrated college and was going away one weekend with the school. He came downstairs on the morning he was leaving with a Glasgow Rangers top on and I told him to take it off. He wasn't going on the trip with a Glasgow Rangers top on. So he said to me, "But all my friends will be wearing tops. What's the difference?" He said, "Why did you send me to an integrated school?" I said that I'd sent him to an integrated school to understand other people and to learn about them and be able to tolerate them. He replied, "Exactly. They're going to have to tolerate that I'm a Glasgow Rangers supporter." I told him to go up the stairs and take the shirt off.

He returned back down the stairs with a Blackburn Rovers shirt on. A Blackburn Rovers shirt is blue and white with an English red rose right in the middle of it. What could I say? I didn't think that anybody in the school would find it offensive, but I'd thought they'd have found the Rangers shirt offensive.

So I drove Christopher to school, and when I drove into the school, all his mates were standing there waiting, and I stopped the car, and he just looked at me. There was five of them. Two of them were wearing Celtic shirts, one was wearing a Cliftonville shirt, and the other two were wearing a Linfield and a Rangers shirt. When he opened the car door to get out, he turned to me and said, "You see? I might not like those football teams. I may be opposed to them, but I recognise that the people wearing the shirts are human beings."

So I learned a lesson. The whole thing about integrated education, about bringing people together, should be about tolerating what the other person is, and understanding that because the other person is different, it doesn't make him an animal.

Billy

Blue Shirts
Green Shirts

My story is about a time when I was a first year and I went over the town with my mum to get new clothes for my holidays. I was wearing my new Rangers top that I got with the money I was given for Easter. I was wearing it under a sweatshirt so I didn't think anyone would really notice.

My mum and I went into Sports Division to get shorts and T-shirts. I couldn't decide which ones I wanted so my mum went ahead into Marks & Spencers until I decided. As soon as my mum was gone, I felt somebody grab my shirt collar. I turned round to see a tall boy with dyed blonde hair and an earring. He said to me, "Hey boy, you don't want to wear that top round here." Then three other boys appeared behind him and they all seemed to be wearing green tops, hats and scarves. They took me into the car park of Foyleside and threw me against the back wall. The bigger boy lifted me up by the neck and kneed me in the privates and I fell to the ground in pain. A woman came and stopped and stared me straight in my eyes which were streaming out tears and she just turned her head and walked on. Then a man who worked in the car park chased the boys away. I couldn't understand why the woman didn't do anything but turned her head.

Would she have helped me if she didn't see my shirt?

David, aged 13

The First Soldier

What actually did happen in the end, was one sunny day this tank arrived at the top of the New Lodge Road. And the strange thing about it was, it wasn't green, it wasn't the normal army colours, it was yellow; like a khaki yellow, the sort of thing you'd expect to see in the desert. It had rolled along the Antrim Road and just turned and faced the New Lodge.

Now there were barricades, literally every couple of yards. So we're sort of looking up to this thing, wondering what's coming, because if they start shooting out of that, we're in trouble. It sat there for hours, and nobody could figure out why it was sitting there. You couldn't see into it. Nobody got out of it. Nobody came near it. No other soldiers. Nothing. There wasn't even a helicopter in the sky. And after it had sat there for a long time, it started to move, but it literally moved at less than walking pace. It came to the first barricade, and it went through it as if it was tissue paper. It just crushed it and came on down the road. People panicked and sort of ran up different streets and whatever. It didn't speed up and nothing came behind it. It just rolled on down the road, taking out every barricade as it met them.

But by the time it had taken out a few of the barricades, it had passed side streets, so there were people now behind it. And someone noticed that on the back door of the tank there was two handles that came out, two steel handles. So that was a weakness. By now there were people all over it and around it, throwing stones at it, and I don't know what else they were trying to do to it. But someone jammed a piece of wood or metal into these two handles which meant that whoever was in it, now couldn't get out of it. The next thing someone else noticed was that there was a fire extinguisher taped onto the side of it and a periscope type thing on the top of it that was turning. Someone took the fire extinguisher off and started to spray the periscope with foam. All of a sudden, from going very straight and very, very slow, it started to sway about the road. The guy driving it obviously couldn't see where he was going anymore.

Then another sort of a panic set in, because this was going to go through a house. If it had, it would have gone straight through the house. I don't know how he did it, and we couldn't see at the time how he could see out, but he managed to get it sort of straight again and it kept going.

By now it had been petrol bombed. It was on fire. It kept on going at the same speed. It went straight through all the barricades. It went straight down and out the other end of the road up North Queen Street where it was met by other soldiers. The door opened and out came these soldiers coughing their lungs up. Nobody was hurt, but what it had proved I think, was that it took one vehicle to open that road, not a regiment of soldiers – nobody shot – just one vehicle.

So that meant the army was back in the road and that was a real downer. It was bad because we didn't know what was going to happen next. Are the army going to come in? This internment thing, are all young men going to be taken away? What's going to happen? It was a frightening time. The army took over the streets, and every now and again one was shot at or one was blown up.

I mean, the first soldier ever shot dead was shot on the New Lodge Road.

Philip

Short extract from 'Night Rider' (a sixty-minute video documentary recording a Belfast taxi driver's memories of the troubles. Produced by An Crann *The Tree 1999).*

A Soldier's Impression of the Creggan

Months after Bloody Sunday and the smashed barricades of Motorman, I arrived on the Creggan with the Grenadier Guards. A sombre mood of despondency hung over the estate like a dark cloud and the run-down old factory in Blighs Lane, where we stayed, seemed to compound the effect. They crammed us like sardines, platoon by platoon into makeshift, partitioned sections under a leaking roof where we were visited by the odd scaly-tailed rodent. I shared a rickety metal bunk with Nikko, who lusted for his girlfriend back home. To the occupants at the top of the hill, Blighs Lane camp must have been like a collection of festering warts on the face of a friend. It was a hastily-constructed fortress of corrugated metal, surrounded by miles of jagged, rusting barbed wire.

The average squaddie, if I was anything to go by, was an immature 19 year old, selfishly engrossed in the insularity of army life, who paid little attention to news and current affairs. The regiment represented a microcosm of the big wide world outside. What any of us knew about Ireland could be written on a pinhead. So we parroted the usual platitudes about representing the rule of law and keeping the warring factions apart. Yet it was plain to see that in Derry there was no overt sectarian conflict between Protestants and Catholics. The natural barrier of the River Foyle separated them, although an incident during my first patrol made me realise how deeply ingrained the conflict was.

Four of us had been moving slowly and self-consciously along Creggan Broadway, resplendent in our shiny new flak vests with rifles held firmly, ready for the first sucker wanting to mess with us. Instead, we were met by a motley tribe of young, stone-throwing Cregganites. A toddler crawled along the pavement, inches from me – the target. As stones landed around us, a piece of paving slab just missed him. I bent down and asked, "Are you alright, little fella?" He screwed his face into a grimace, raised his little hand and made a V-sign. Then I heard the crash of a door as mum came charging down the path like a rhino, bust bouncing, her face flame red and fists tightly clenched. She screamed, "Fuck off limey and leave my wee nadger alone." Shocked, I turned back to keep an eye on the stone-throwers, just in time to see a big round boulder bounce off the pavement and smash into my shin. Inadvertently, the pain caused me to let out a wimpish yelp. The kids loved it and showed their appreciation by cheering as I limped down the street, pursued by the neighbourhood mongrels barking and snapping at my heels. I felt stupid and soon realised that showing concern was naively misplaced. It was a jungle and I had better wise up. It also dawned on me that a rifle, flak vest and ammo were no answer to the sheer bloody hatred I saw in the eyes of that embryonic little republican.

The pressure of living in a small Portakabin with twenty or so other blokes took its toll. It made me selfish and out for number one. Sod the heroics, just stay sharp and focused to get back home in one piece. That was my sole aim. Most evenings, as the sun turned into a giant orange orb before sinking over the horizon, the young guns of the IRA would loose off a few rounds from Central Drive, as if to emphasise a point. One evening it triggered a gun battle, where we fired two hundred rounds. The only victims were the residents of Creggan Heights, whose houses were riddled like colanders. One family sitting inno-cently watching TV got the fright of their lives as their screen disintegrated after bullets fired from the camp poured through it. Miraculously, no-one was injured or killed.

We nicknamed one gunman 'Mints', who drove us to distraction all summer with his well-rehearsed one-shot sniping. Crack! And off he went, handing the armalite to his buddies who stripped it down, shared the parts around and got the girls to hide them under skirts, jackets, prams and shopping bags. Each time Mints was arrested, he was let out, due to his age – 15. Try, reader, to imagine our sheer frustration at a cocky kid

trying to take your life with as much compassion as a motorist squashing a hedgehog. So it was no small wonder when at times we took the law into our own hands. Right or wrong.

On one patrol, we turned the corner on to Central Drive and immediately felt the tension. It was like entering a room of people and knowing they were talking about you. Old women in the bus queue were shoved aside by young girls, then came a whiplash crack! The next sound came from my own rifle – as if on autopilot I felt the butt in my shoulder and fired. The shot went in the opposite direction. It didn't matter as long as it made the bastard think twice about shooting at us again. My tracer round carved an arch before taking a chunk of masonry out of the top of Cromore flats. The fear of military discipline helped me quickly invent a story about a gunman firing from that location. Fortunately, during the follow-up operation, Nikko uncovered an armalite in a coal shed complete with a full magazine of rounds and telescopic sight.

One Christmas, a rare event occurred, as the four of us loped out of base, past the jeering faces of Blighs Lane factory workers. A brown-haired, middle-aged woman strode purposefully towards us, impervious to the aerial bombardment that we came under from the kids grouped at the top of the hill. As we passed she patted each of us on the back, and said in a cheery voice, "Merry Christmas and God Bless youse boys." That small thing amazed me. I later wondered what had made her do such a thing. Had she seen past the uniform to see us for what we really were, just snotty-nosed kids with big rifles? Boys like her own sons, perhaps? It was easy to like the people of the Creggan who went quietly about their lives, not trying to kill us and endeavouring, against the odds, to raise their families decently. They were truly the salt of the earth.

The peace process renewed my interest in Ireland and I felt a strong draw to go back, look around and try to understand what the conflict had been about. I was fed up with reading books and doing the odd evening course. It was time to go back and see for myself. Initially it was my intention to explore Belfast first, but driving off the ferry I was drawn towards Derry like a moth to a flame. As I drove over Craigavon Bridge, the old town had a vaguely familiar feel, parts still dilapidated and world-weary, mixed with modern developments. The signs led me up to the Creggan, once a strange, hostile place to anyone in uniform. Gone were Cromore flats where my shot gouged out a chunk of masonry, gone too were the old dreaded Central Drive shops and flats. The houses on the estate had been given a face-lift. It was a totally rejuvenated estate, that looked nothing like the way I remembered it.

I drove on to the city cemetery to seek out Mints, sure he'd be lying under six foot of Irish soil, the recipient of British lead. Two hours passed, alone up there on the hill searching for him. I didn't find his name etched on a piece of stone and was glad. Seriously. I was told later that he was working over in England sending back money to his family. The dour, grey-stoned republican plot conveyed to me the message of eternal suffering and struggle; the culture of the victim where history lives and no injustice is ever forgotten. Trouble is, it becomes self-perpetuating, as endless rows of stones in a graveyard bear testimony. Many of the names on the Roll of Honour were familiar from the books and papers I had read over the last few years. Such a waste.

Again, I struggled to believe that all those years ago, in a minor way, I had been involved in this ancient conflict too and I had been the enemy. I felt a strange affinity with the dead young men who came from parents as poor as mine, a sort of class-consciousness or empathy for the underdog. Under the skin we were not that different. If I had been born in a republican household on the Creggan, met with inequality and the bone-headed intransigence of Ulster Unionism, maybe I too would have tried to join the IRA. With a mixture of emotions, I paid my respects to the dead of Bloody Sunday; innocents shot by Paras, soldiers of the British army, same as me. That made me angry and sad.

Later in the week I stood in County Donegal on the Bloody Foreland, looking out over the Atlantic. I felt something akin to a spiritual affinity to the wild spirit and soft, undulating beauty of dear old Mother Ireland and its tragic human history. In another of those brief moments of insight, it became clearer why the young men of the IRA had their names etched on gravestones. It felt right that I was back. Now it was time to learn, and in some humble way, assist in the healing process. I fought back tears and prayed like thousands of others over the last thirty years that the madness was finally coming to an end. I believe it is. God Bless.

Mick

Friday, 7 April 1972

I was at work on a building site when I was told there was a phone call for me to get home quick, as there had been a serious explosion on the estate where I lived. A mate gave me a lift home. Soldiers of the Parachute Regiment stopped us some distance from home. After producing ID, I was allowed to proceed on foot. Groups of people were standing about very agitated. There was a heavy, unpleasant odour in the air. I found my wife and asked her the obvious questions. She told me of hearing an awful bang, seeing the cloud of smoke at the end of the estate, and running down to see what had happened.

Near the site of the explosion there were pieces of human remains lying about with steam rising from them. When I arrived, firemen were collecting human remains from gardens and rooftops, and I could see a young paratrooper crying and being comforted by a mate. However, I found that no soldier had been injured, but three youths from the estate were missing, and three garages destroyed.

One youth was identified on the spot, this was Samuel Hughes. He was dead. Later we were to find that our son Jack McErlean, 17 years was one of the dead, as was Charles McCrystal, 17 years.

At the mortuary next morning, only Sammy Hughes was identified, the rest was just pieces of flesh and bone with a human tongue on top. Why we were asked by police to view these remains I don't know. Perhaps we were being given an object lesson. But about what?

Jack

I was reared believing…

the republican government had an army across the border waiting to come over and kill us in our beds. I believed that all Catholics were bad, were there to do us harm, and got involved in a local paramilitary organisation when I was 16 years of age. In my time, I was responsible for intimidating a lot of Catholic families that I grew up with and who lived in my area. During my time, I put a bomb through someone's letter box. I put a bomb beneath a van because I believed that the guy that drove the van was a Provisional IRA man. I later found out he wasn't, and lucky enough,

the bomb didn't go off. I went through life believing that I was the defender of the faith and defender of the community.

One night, my friends brought a young man to my door because they thought he was a Catholic. It was an October night and dark; a fairly bad night near Hallowe'en. I was having my supper when the knock came to the door and when I opened it one of my friends said, "Sam, we found this guy walking down the street. We think he's a Taig." I asked him who he was and where he was from and what he was

doing there. He told us he had escaped from Magilligan prison and had ended up round where I lived. He was in for car theft and only had another two months to go, when someone drove into the prison and left the keys in a car. He and his mate jumped into the car and drove to the gate. The prison officer opened the two gates and they drove out and I thought, 'Aye, right, Jack.' We decided to take him up a path and shoot him.

We took him to a place

called the Snaky Path, a windy path that runs up through the estate along the side of the houses and has no lights. Three of us had gone with one gun, and I was thinking, 'Let's get this over with.' When we got up the path to where it was dark, we got him on his knees and put the gun to the back of his head, and I was thinking, 'Just do it and get it over with. I can't lose face to these two guys.' When we were about to shoot him, we discovered that his name was King, who were a pretty big family living on the Sandy Row at that time. We took him back down to my house. My mother heard the commotion and got up out of bed and came down wanting to know what was going on. We never told her everything – that we were going to shoot him. She proceeded to make soup and sandwiches for the guy before he went home. I was trying to act throughout all this as the cool guy, but I can remember my nerves. I was shaking.

We got him to Sandy Row after his soup, where he survived for two months before being caught. He ended up going back to jail and serving a further six months for breaking out of custody and he only had another two months to do of his sentence. That was the closest I ever came to shooting or taking someone's life. It haunts me in a lot of ways; the vision of this fella on his knees, and me standing with a gun to the back of his head is always in my head. I can't forget about it. I was so close, and lucky that somebody came up and recognised him and said, "Yes, I know your father." That was the only thing that saved him. After that, and the suspended sentence for possession of arms, I began to look out for people in my own local community. I began working in the local youth club and started to look and think about things in different ways.

Getting the suspended sentence kept the paramilitaries off my back. I'd have been a security risk if I'd been active. The police would have wanted to watch me. I started to question things, to ask why, rather than just accepting what someone says. That was a big thing at that time, because you weren't meant to ask questions. You weren't meant to ask why. You were just meant to go and do it, partly because you were brought up to listen to and respect your elders and not answer them back. I became a thorn in the flesh of certain people's sides because I was trying to provide alternatives for young people, rather than going along with the rest of the sheep. The UDA at one stage took me away in a car and dropped me off in a place called the Knock Monument, which is up above Monkstown, and beat me up with pickaxe handles that at that time were baseball bats. They left me there with no shoes or socks on and I had to walk home. I can remember the police's attitude at the time. I was walking down the road in my bare feet and they gave me a lift. They were more concerned with what I had done to deserve it. Did I rob somewhere? Are you prepared to make a statement against these people? That kind of shocked me at the time.

I went across the border for the first time eight or nine years ago and the first time I went across the border I thought, 'Is this right? Am I doing the right thing? Am I turning colours by going across the border?' Because the way I was reared from when I was eight years old was, as I say, to believe they were waiting across the border to come across and murder us in our beds. That's the way the Unionist Party wanted us to believe. That's how the Unionist Party survived so long. That's how Paisley survived so long.

Sam

Footsteps

The sound of feet walking on pavements is something not usually heard in the city. Too many other sounds constantly harass the ears. Yet when I think of Belfast during the troubles, it is that sound which brings it all into sharp focus. People walking, people running, people marching, the sound of their footsteps mingling and growing, sometimes purposefully, sometimes in panic. The sound, for me, became the theme tune of the strife.

We woke early on a morning in August 1971 to silence. A tense, nervous silence. We tuned to the radio. Internment, fires, riots had all happened during the night. There was no traffic. All public transport had been cancelled. We lived three miles from the city centre and not more than two from a so-called republican area where no-one had slept that night. My daughter and I decided to walk together to work to see how far we could get. As we began our journey, our heels rang out on the paving stones and echoed back from the buildings in the silent streets. Other feet were walking too, the sound of our footsteps underlining the complete absence of traffic noise.

As we came to where the riots had taken place, we were engulfed in smoke. We saw flames reaching into the sky from the fiercely blazing buildings and strewn rubble everywhere.

The numbers walking had now swollen to a crowd. We were redirected to avoid areas where gunfire was continuing. We walked on and then a soldier told us that if we were determined to go on, we had better run for it. We ran for it.

Since then, so many troubles, so many silences, so many walking feet.

On the Sunday when Ian Paisley defied the ban on marches and led his members up the Woodstock Road, the army broke up the march with tear gas. As the marchers stampeded, the sound of those running feet was terrifying, like a tidal wave sweeping all before it.

There was the Saturday when shopping in Donegall Place was stopped by a UDA march through the city. The traffic stopped and the footsteps stamped defiance. We stood watching, some people waving and clapping, but most with expressionless faces, hiding private thoughts.

The silence during the UUUC strike when footsteps in the street could be the forerunner of some violent activity, or a neighbour hurrying home to safety.

Then one weekend came when the women said,

'Enough is enough,' and they walked – how they walked! Women came from everywhere. They swept down from the Falls Road and the Shankill Road. They came from the east, west, north, and south. They marched eight-deep down the Ormeau Road into Ormeau Park where they met another great mass swinging in from the embankment. They met and hugged and laughed and wept. Old friends met and new friends were made.

We felt that a movement was born that day which must succeed. We were given the energy and the will. We were fired with determination and elated with the power and strength of our convictions. Much was done, but the dying and needless suffering continued. Since then we have walked to many peace demonstrations and services.

There is a kind of magic in starting out from home and being joined by more and more people along the way, until the footsteps are beating out the tattoo – sending out the message:

 'Stop the killing, stop the terror! Peace! Peace! Peace!'

Eva

Kids at Play

Kids with sticks,
  came running down the hill,
from the 'other side',
  the dark side of the moon,
for all we knew or cared.
  We turned and ran
back up the hill
  to our side.
Because we didn't
  understand their war,
not yet anyway.

We went back
  to our park,
but it wasn't half
  as much fun.
They had bigger, faster slides.
  That's discrimination!

They've built a wall now,
  in the middle of Alexandra Park.
A Peace Line
  to separate the kids at play.
and fathers at war.

It's sad
  when the price of peace,
is a twenty-foot wall.

Mark

The Field Trip

My friends and I were so excited that morning. The bus arrived at the school and we all started out on our field trip. Things went well. We collected all sorts of flowers and other pieces of materials for our school project.

By three o'clock we were nearly home. The bus suddenly stopped at the Brook Road. I was feeling strange. 'What has happened?' I said to myself. We were re-routed and the bus arrived at the school. I can't remember who told me, but someone said that a bomb had just exploded in Conlan's bar. I felt very frightened and I started to shake because I knew something terrible had happened to my father, who I knew was in the bar.

I just started running and never stopped until I was outside the bar. My heart was racing. 'My God, where is he? I can't see him.' The dust and smoke was everywhere. I panicked, pulling at bricks and pieces of debris, this screaming going on in my head. I was pulled away by someone and they told me that everything would be all right.

I felt sad then because I knew that this wasn't true. My father had been taken away in an ambulance so I decided to stay with my mother who was standing by the roadside with the priest and the manager of the bar.

They arranged to take my mother home, so I walked down the road, knowing in my heart that my daddy was dead. I went into our house and saw my mother just sitting there with a neighbour standing beside her and my brothers and sisters sitting on the sofa. My mother looked so sad and lonely. "It's all right," I said to her. "Someone told me that my daddy has hurt his legs." "No," my mother said. "Your daddy is dead." My mind went blank and I took my youngest brother on my knee and started rocking with him. I felt sad and lonely and so alone. "No, no, all this isn't true," I burst out, "He's only hurt his legs. The other man told me so."

I felt so empty. 'What are we going to do? I want my daddy.' These words kept coming back to me. 'Please God make him be all right.' But that was not to be.

When I close my eyes as if to blink, I see your face in front of me. I don't know why you went away. But I know in my heart that I loved you and wanted you to stay.

Mary

When I was at my most militant loyalist stage...

I met Tommy, who was a Catholic. I met him on the dodgems in Barry's amusements in Portrush. I was 17 and on my first ever trip away from home on my own. Two weeks after I met him, he asked me to marry him and I agreed to do that, but we couldn't, because we had this huge dilemma of where we should marry and what we should do because of the Catholic-Protestant thing. We used to spend hours thinking about it, trying to find something we had in common and we never could find anything we had in common. Our views were so opposed.

The estate I grew up in was 95 per cent Protestant and I don't remember ever having been in contact with a Catholic before Tommy. My family were a very loyalist family. My father was in the Orange Order and the Black Institution and the Masonic. As children, we were never taught any anti-Catholic stuff. My parents would have been very sure of their own convictions, particularly my father. But he never spoke against Catholicism. We were never taught to hate. We were just taught that this is what we are and you accept everybody else for being what they are as well. We were always told we had to vote unionist, that it was very important, but we were never told why it was important. It was just what we did. So I never questioned anything – it's just what we did.

Tommy's family was very nationalist, especially his father. He actually threw me out of the house at one stage and said he didn't want Tommy to bring me back again because I was saying I didn't want to marry in the Catholic Church. I wasn't prepared to do that, so we really didn't know what to do. In the end, we didn't marry for three years, until Tommy was 21 and didn't need the consent of his parents anymore.

Tommy's daddy didn't know he was getting married. He thought he'd gone camping with some of his friends for the weekend. In Blackpool, we wrote him a letter and told him we'd got married the Saturday before, that we were sorry to have hurt him and really hoped that he would understand. After that, we didn't see him for three years.

We married in the Church of Ireland in 1970, a time when the country had just erupted and gone mad. Everyone was telling us that there was absolutely no future for mixed marriages. The minister that married us in the Church of Ireland also told me I was mad, that I'd taken leave of my senses.

My family liked Tommy and were very supportive because I was marrying in a Protestant Church. I know if I'd told them I was going to marry in a Catholic Church, their reaction would have been just as strong as Tommy's family, so I didn't blame his family. I knew where they were coming from.

All of my family were at the wedding, as well as Tommy's young sister who was only 14 or 15 at the time. Tommy's mummy came to the house the day before the wedding and I showed her my dress and all the wedding presents. She was very upset because she wouldn't be able to come, but she knew she couldn't because of the way things were with Tommy's father.

After we were married, Tommy would go down to his mother's house during the day when he knew his father would be out at work. That cost him a lot, for he and his father had had a good relationship and he loved his father very much. It wasn't like there were problems at home or anything. He had been happy at home and happy with his family.

The way the country was in the early 1970s, we weren't sure where we were going to live. We couldn't live on my old estate because of the mixed marriage thing and weren't very confident of living anywhere. Eventually, we were offered a flat right at the top of a multi-storey in Rathcoole, right across the street from Tommy's mummy and daddy. We thought we could be reasonably anonymous there with us both out working all day. We never bothered with people and they never bothered with us. But then I got pregnant, and we knew we were going to have to look for a house. Tommy also lost his job.

We were sitting at home one night, when our door rapped. It was Tommy's daddy. It was the first time we'd seen him since before the wedding. We discovered that his mother over the years had gradually begun to inform him of how we were doing. He came into the house and said, "What's this I hear about you being paid off? Go over and get your coat. There's a fella I know works in the shipyard and he says if you come round, he'll see if he can get you started." So away he went, and there wasn't another word. It was his way. He was never going to sit and talk about it or sit and discuss what had gone on. And that was it. From that night on he was fine.

When our first child was born, Tommy's mum and dad were delighted because she was the first grandchild, for both sides of the family. And nobody ever discussed the fact that she was being brought up a Protestant. It was never discussed. We never discussed it at all. We just learned to talk on a level that didn't offend anybody. It was all a bit superficial, but it was the only way we could deal with it.

Jean

The Orange Field

Belfast was never a town I liked, and yet I chose it for a marathon walk. Early during the walk at the Westlink, before we reached the Shankill and the Falls, there were armoured cars, police and army. We walked on, thought nothing of it. This was Belfast after all. Later, back home, friends asked where the walk had to go. We had been re-routed and didn't even know. This set me to thinking for the first time in many years about the Orange Field.

Every third year the parades came. In June my brother and I would climb the iron gate or the high, drystone wall. My biggest fear of Orangemen was that they would not have cleared the field of cows in early June and we would land with a splat on a cow-pat. Then I would round on my brother and tell him this year he had got it wrong, there would be no parades. The men wouldn't come and sit here in cow shite. If the field was clear then I knew that they would come this year with their bright orange sashes, banners and bands. They'd march through the town in July which in childhood summers was always full of blazing light.

The Orange Field is a lovely field – flat at the top as you enter the gate and falling down to the river Roe in a long, slow sweep. The river bank along the length of the field is full of small beaches of shingle and sand which shift from year to year. We swam there on warm summer days.

The field was there for us to enjoy as well and I skipped along behind the bands, giggling about neighbours, who were staggering drunk, in their bowler hats and sashes. There was one boy who took offence if you mentioned this.

I knew we were not Orange, yet had no idea that some of those who *were* perceived me as something which I was not. That realisation came much later – I left, unsure, and encountered some in Dublin, who spoke their *cúpla focail* – 'Don't you have any Irish? Ah, but, of course, you're

from the North.' I am indeed an Irish woman from the North where bodhran, whistle, flute and Lambeg drum are played with joy.

My daughters are now big enough to clamber over the wrought-iron gate or the wall which has been painted red, white and blue at the top. The little one says, "There's the Spice Girl flag," when she sees the Union Jack. I wonder if that boy from long ago would take offence at that.

On hot summer days we go and picnic in the Orange Field. Fly down the long curve of grass, arms outstretched, whooping with delight, until we reach a sandy cove on the banks of the Roe. The field is still there to be enjoyed.

Debbie

Token Gestures

Extract from a short drama for one actress

We have a great command of language, in this country.
How we use it shows our own perspective.
Someone's freedom fighter is another person's terrorist.
Derry/Londonderry. Fire/Dogma…

It's like this – I've heard it said that nationalists have a fire burning within them.
A fire. Now, I take it that is what they believe in.
That's what gives them their identity and for which they feel a passion.
OK.
But how is it that what I believe in…my fire, is portrayed as dogma steeped in bigotry?

What makes their fire different from mine?

And why do those resentful Ulstermen,
those ones who have gained some respectability in their field,
stand and in their broad Ulster vowels say…

'I see myself as an Irishman.'

Like, yeah. I see myself as six feet tall and looking like Cindy Crawford
but saying it doesn't make it true.

It's just that, well, every time someone from my neck of the woods says things like that,
it's as if they deny the heritage held by me and others like me.
Like that saying, 'Give Ireland back to the Irish'.
The bit that comes after that reads,
'And fuck the rest of 'em'.
I used that word – Ulster.
Using it makes you stand out – as if you're staunch, or something.

Many people dilute it saying 'Northern Ireland.'
Not 'Ireland', mind you.
God no. You don't want to be seen to be Irish!
So you say, 'Northern Ireland.'

A respected Ulster poet apparently declared something along the line of:

"I'm an Ulsterman of Planter stock.
I was born in the island of Ireland, so secondly I'm an Irishman.
I was born in the British archipelago and English is my native tongue, so I am British.
The British archipelago are offshore islands to the continent of Europe, so I'm European."

Now, some people would say he was an apologist of an Ulsterman.
Others could say he was far-seeing, far-reaching.
Me?
What's in the back of my mind is that we could consider ourselves Martians
'cos we exist in the same solar system as Mars.

Those men, those ones who have got the camera's eye, disappoint me.
They stand, and in their broad Ulster vowels say,
'I see myself as an Irishman.'
They become dividers then.

They divide their audience straight down the middle.

Have I done that? Have I divided the audience?

I needed this space…this centre stage.

Anne

What type of people would have you beaten off the road just so they can march...?

It seems to me that their whole parade is about totally ignoring the sensitivities of the people in the area that I live in. Because these people are marching, it means that I can not physically cross the road. I get trapped in an area which on the one side is bound by the river, and on the other side, by the road which is full of marchers. My big problem is the fact that they feel they're entitled to close the road off to come marching through an area where they're obviously not wanted or welcome and when they themselves don't offer me the same rights. The majority of the people in my area are Catholic and wouldn't even be allowed to join the Orange Order. They wouldn't be accepted. If they married somebody that was in the Orange Order, then that person would be kicked out. They would disbar their members if they went to a Catholic Church service. I mean, I could become a unionist, or I could become a Presbyterian, but I wouldn't be allowed to join the Orange Order because I'm contaminated by having Catholic parents and having been baptised a Catholic. That makes me totally unacceptable. I believe that any organisation that behaves in that way and has that type of attitude to people shouldn't be afforded the rights to just march wherever they want, or when they want, even if that's only once a year. I feel it's totally unacceptable. I accept that they're allowed to exist. You can't stop people being bigots but you don't have to allow them to parade their bigotry. I mean, if it was the Ku Klux Klan, I don't think the black areas in America would have to accept the Ku Klux Klan marching through their streets. Their whole attitude would strike me as being extremely racist. They're saying that people that are Catholics are a different type of person from themselves.

At first I didn't get involved in the protests. I work in a power station and felt that for me to be out there standing protesting, with what would have been only a few people at the very beginning, would have made me look like some sort of republican activist. People from the Ormeau Road are painted as being republican, and people think the demonstrations are all republican but I don't see it like that. It's a demonstration of people who are saying that they don't agree with people who are bigots marching and parading. Then the bookies incident happened, when five people were shot dead. After that a lot of people were willing to go out and protest, and I felt it was a good idea and that I should too and lend a hand to it. The IRA called a ceasefire, and it was felt you could do a legitimate, peaceful protest without the thing turning into violence.

The tension was very high in the area after the shooting. There was a lot of bitterness and anger about it and a lot of distrust of the police and army. There was a permanent police checkpoint only a minute away from the bookies where the shooting took place, about seven hundred yards, and yet no-one was caught. It takes more than one minute to shoot five people dead, so people began to suspect collusion. At that time, I thought the Orange Order might have made some sort of gesture and say they wouldn't come down the road, but they didn't and the protests increased and succeeded in stopping some of the parades. In an attempt to get good communication going between the Residents' Association and the Orange Order, there was an agreement to let one of the marches come down the road one Saturday morning. One of the bands playing in the march was a UVF band and I thought it was a bit rich that the UVF was on the drum

and it was the UVF that claimed responsibility for the shooting in the bookies. It was a UVF band linked to the Ulster Volunteer Force that fought in the battle of the Somme in the First World War, not the same as the one who did the killing, but I still felt that was just a wee bit of salt being rubbed in the wound. They both have the same origins and were set up to maintain a Protestant Ulster, that's what it was all about. It was, 'Ulster will fight and Ulster will be right', that was the philosophy of Carson. It struck me anyway, that it was a bit rich for them to be parading after the shooting.

The thing is but, my knowledge of the Orange Order is limited. Maybe if they could educate me and show me they're not this organisation which is anti-Catholic, that they're an organisation that embraces Catholics joining them, then I wouldn't have a problem. There was one year there was an agreement made which would have allowed them two marches down the Ormeau Road, and then they were to come down and meet us and find out about our community and we were to go and meet them and find out about their community. Then one of their representatives said that this wasn't an agreement that was binding to the Orange Order, but had been between one member of the Orange Order and the Residents' Association. The man who made the agreement then said he couldn't guarantee that he would even be in the Orange Order the next year, so people felt that without some sort of total assurances, they weren't going to keep their word. It ended up nothing happened. People protested and they marched and they've continued to march ever since. I think the agreement would have been a good agreement, because it would have been a good thing for people to have learned about each other, and see where their truth lies and where their falseness lies. Because I don't know. My perception is that the Orange Order are bigots, anti-Catholics, but maybe I'm wrong, you know? If I'm wrong, I'd like to be proved wrong. People can change.

Dominic

I suppose I should start off by introducing myself. My name is Susan, and I come from the Shankill Road. I was born in Joseph Street, locally known as the Banjo. Don't ask me why, but that was how it was known. We lived in a little kitchen house with two bedrooms, and with four boys and four girls in the family, you can imagine it was pretty crowded. My father worked in the Central Library as an attendant, and of course the money was a bit scarce on the ground with so many mouths to feed. We couldn't afford holidays like today's generation, whose holidays are a must, but we were pretty content with our lot.

The highlight of our lives was Christmas, and of course, the Eleventh night and the Twelfth day. My father was a member of the Orange Order and the Black Institution and went to his meetings regularly. I don't know exactly when he joined both institutions, but neither do I remember when he wasn't a member. We were brought up in a Christian home, and attended church and Sunday school regularly. We looked forward mostly to the Eleventh and Twelfth because there always seemed to be a happy atmosphere about the whole district. In fact, it was more like a carnival atmosphere. People put up arches and decorated their houses and the streets, and there was lots of music and bands about. Friends would drop in at all times to visit. Sometimes someone you hadn't seen for years would suddenly come to visit. We gathered wood for the bonfires, and to me it seemed like a good way to get rid of a lot of household waste, and it didn't cost anything. Then when the bonfires were lit, people would dance and sing and have a good time. Then on the Twelfth morning, my mother would get up and make sure that my father had a good breakfast as he had a long walk in front of him to the Field. Once my father was gone, the rest of the family would be washed and dressed and head up to Clifton Street to watch the Orangemen parade to Finaghy.

When I was 14, I met a boy who was to become my husband and he came from the same type of background as myself. He was a member of the Junior Orange Order. His father and all his brothers were also members. They used to have social nights, and of course, I was invited along, and I always had a good time as there was a good

A Personal Statement

atmosphere and people there were just generally enjoying themselves. I then started to go to outings with them, and when I was old enough, I went to the Field on the twelfth of July with a few chums. We would dance to the bands, sometimes the whole way there and back.

Then in 1951, a friend asked me if I would like to join her ladies' lodge, and I said yes. When I went I once again enjoyed a very happy atmosphere and great companionship as it was more like a social club. Once I joined, it just never seemed to enter my head not to go, as I felt I would be missing something. During the time I have been in the Order, I have acted as Treasurer, Chaplain, Deputy Mistress and then Mistress in 1960 for three years, and I felt very proud to be in that position. As the years went on, I was elected to an office in my district lodge, and eventually became District Mistress of Number Four Ladies' Lodge four years ago, and I still hold that position and I consider it to be a great honour. During the years I was in my own lodge, my mother also joined and remained a member until she died in 1978. When the ladies' lodges were invited by the Brethren to join them in the parades, I felt so proud as I felt I was doing something that my father had done for so many years, and I suppose in a way I wanted to follow in his footsteps. It is a pity he is not alive today to see me when I walk proudly ahead of the ladies on the Twelfth day, and at all the church services which we attend.

The only thoughts I have when I am out on parade are to enjoy the atmosphere and the companionship of all my friends, and the furthest thought from all our minds is to hurt or annoy anybody in any way, as we just want to celebrate – whatever the occasion. Both my husband and I have worked with Roman Catholics all our lives, and we have always got on very well with them. One of my closest friends was a girl from McDonnell Street, off Albert Street, Falls Road, and she came from a very staunch Catholic family, and even today when we meet in the town we embrace each other like long-lost relatives. My husband has retired just over two years as a domestic supervisor in the Royal Victoria Hospital, and he had 28 of a staff – all women and 25 of them were Roman Catholics. When we meet them they are very happy to see him and say how they wish he was still their boss. In fact, they make a point of watching for him on the Twelfth day.

I just can't understand how the parades have been going on all these years, and they were enjoyed by both sides of the community, and now that we have a so-called ceasefire, they have suddenly become so offensive to the other community. I can assure you I don't go out to bother anyone as I was always brought up to believe everyone was entitled to their opinion, and I have never tried to influence anyone away from their beliefs which they have been brought up with, so I cannot see that I am doing any harm to anyone, and I cannot understand why anyone should want to harm me just because I am a Protestant, and proud to be one. I feel there is a very small minority of the Roman Catholic population who object to the Orange Order, and as we all know it only takes a little fire to start a pot boiling. If something bothered me so much as an Orange parade seems to do to some people, I would not go out of my way to watch it, which is what a lot of the objectors seem to do.

Susan

She had only known the prison walls...

She didn't know cars. She didn't know flowers. She didn't know swans. She didn't know birds. She didn't know the things that other children know from when they're born. All of that was totally new to her.

I was getting married that summer when we were lifted and so the wedding was initially cancelled. Whenever I got bail and was out again, I got pregnant. It was one of them things that happened. When I was imprisoned in 1985, I was by that time married with a six week old daughter. Five of us had been arrested, and we all went to Armagh Prison after spending seven days at Castlereagh.

All my friends went to A-wing, which was where all the political prisoners were kept. I was put in B-wing, over in another part of the prison. They said I was put there because of safety regulations, because of the child, but this was absolute nonsense because they could have moved me to C-wing if any trouble started. They were able to move me anywhere, upstairs, downstairs. Basically the attitude was, they didn't want the other women political prisoners to have contact with the child. This meant me and my daughter were isolated from the others. I regret not always being with the rest of the women on the wing because there's a sense of comradeship. I was kept on my own, even though I knew I wasn't 'alone'.

I only had a year with my daughter and when they eventually took her away from me, my heart was breaking. At the same time, you couldn't show weakness in any form because it would have been used against you. I couldn't show how I felt, but my heart was literally aching. It was like a death to me. I knew in my heart that she must have been finding it difficult and everybody had said, 'Ach, after a couple of days she'll be all right,' but I knew she wouldn't forget. During those first couple of weeks I knew in my heart and soul she'd been screaming and throwing tantrums because she was a strong-headed child. You know your own children and I'd always seen that in her. I knew all this was going on, but they thought by telling me nothing, I'd have thought everything was fine. They were trying to keep the pain away from me.

It was about six weeks before they could even bring her up to see me. The first time she came in, she wouldn't even look at me. She just kept her head down and refused to acknowledge me, refused to even kiss me, or anything. It was like she was angry with me for hurting her. You knew she was breaking her heart because she'd been so used to being with me. You knew she was feeling hurt and lonely, but God love her. She was really a strong wee thing and she'd done so well for herself, even now. She's that type of child. She's great.

After that first time, she came once a week for half-an-hour. She still held on to some of the small traits of prison. If you were going from cell to cell, you would have put everything in a plastic bag for lock-up, so that everything was together; books you were studying, knitting, sewing, cigarettes and stuff like that. At home she would always have walked about with her plastic bag with everything in it. She had small prison traits like that at home, walking around the house, putting things in plastic bags and carrying them with her. Everywhere she was going, she was packing things into plastic bags. They found that hilarious at home, that she would have been doing the exact same thing. Well, it's not hilarious because kids will do the exact same things as you do. She kept that up for long enough – for long enough she kept that going.

She was three and a half when I came home. I was so fortunate in that I had good family support and back up. My husband was just brilliant and I was very fortunate compared to an awful lot of other people maybe. A lot of other people didn't come home to their families. I was straight into work, into having a house and a home. I just felt a great sense of being needed and I know a lot of other people don't feel that. I didn't even have time to think about what I had just come through in prison and all the other things. I don't know where to begin, to even start dissecting it because it was all probably too much. People are only now beginning to reflect on their grief. I think now they'll start to feel it with everything becoming more steadier. It's like if you could dwell on it or think about it, what will be the outcome of it? Maybe the problems we're facing now are the worst ones and you nearly feel you've no right to start talking until everybody's been heard. Do you understand what I'm saying?

Kathy

Us & Them

I was born in Ballymena where my parents had a paper shop. My father was an actor and entertainer and taught the banjo, mandolin and guitar when he was home. He was also in the ENSA during the war years – that is a concert party whose job it was to entertain the troops.

Nobody asked anybody their religion. We were all in the same boat then, trying to survive. We lived from day to day and let others live.

I remember at the age of 14, taking part in the Mid-Antrim Drama Club's first production. One of our members, a lovely white-haired lady, put her name forward as a parliamentary candidate. Some time later, I said to my mother, "I wish I could vote and I would vote for my friend." I named the lady. My mother's answer was, "You couldn't. She's not your party."

I was mystified.

Kathleen

Holiday Home

Home, Drumcree and violence
is a news item at the breakfast table.
The tides swim away from the shores of Ballymacoda,
the sound of wood pigeons and seagulls
wafting like a secret language of compromise.
It's time to take down the tents and move on,
away from the North,
South, East, and West to Skibbereen.

Across the Cork and Kerry mountains,
the kids elbowed and argued for space
in the back seat. I was trying to stay calm,
composing a poem in my head. How the shifting light
changes drastically on the mountains.
"Look at this boys, it's magic." "What?" they said,
and shot forward from the back seat.
"The scenery," I said. "Oh that," they said,
and elbowed on. The poem disappeared in the tunnel
cut from rock.

The rain beat down on the tent like a Lambeg drum,
and a cold front set in and news of the murder of three
young brothers. Shivers crawled along my spine.
My wife and I huddled in silence
with our three young boys, and the thoughts
of their loss filled the tent. The forecast said
it would rain in Munster, Leinster, and Connaught,
and be fine in Ulster.

I drove through the belting rain to Staige Fort.
I heard someone on the radio portray Drumcree
as a barbecue for families by day
and Hamburger Hill at night.

Home isn't far from our holiday,
and our holiday
isn't far enough from home.

Adrian

Rude Awakening

I used to live on a very one-sided estate in Craigavon. I didn't like it very much as I found the people very unfriendly, and I couldn't understand why all they wanted to talk about all the time was religion. I personally found this very boring, but I learned to put up with it.

While sitting outside my house one summer, I got to know not only a few of the respectable people from the estate, but also a few of the hoods. They would come and chat to me, and pass the time of day. My philosophy on life has always been to take people as you find them, and not to pass judgment until they actually do something to you personally. One hood from the estate often called and would stay for a coffee and a chat, often borrowing a cigarette when he was stuck, or bringing my kids a bag of sweets each. Everybody warned that he was trouble, but as usual I took no notice and welcomed him into my home.

July came and soon the Drumcree siege was upon us. Not wanting to be any part of the warfare that was going on in my estate at the time, my whole family bought a caravan and went to Millisle for the summer season. We only came home once a week, normally on a Sunday night – mainly for me to get my washing done, and to restock on the shopping for the caravan. But one particular Sunday night will always stick in my mind.

The kids went to bed at around their usual time of ten o'clock, and Wayne and I sat down to watch a bit of television and relax. At around twelve we both decided it was time for bed. We checked everywhere was locked up and safe, and headed upstairs. As usual Wayne went to sleep fairly quickly, while I took a little longer to drop off. At around three o'clock, I heard someone banging like mad on my front door. I looked over at Wayne still fast asleep, and thought to myself, 'I'll leave him there.' I crept downstairs to answer the door. I was totally amazed by what I saw. There in front of me was my friendly hood, dressed from top to toe in black. I recognised him immediately but didn't let on.

"What on earth do you want at this time of the morning?"

"Is he in?" came the reply.

"Who? Wayne, of course he is. He's in his bed sleeping along with the rest of my family," I then replied abruptly.

"Well, just go and get him and give him this."

With that he handed me a balaclava, a black one the same as he was wearing at the time.

"Tell him to get out here now. We need all the help we can get. You live on this estate, and now's the time to stand up for our rights, and protect it."

I stood there horrified, my knees felt like jelly, but I knew that I wasn't going to even wake up my husband, let alone get him up to fight. Taking a very deep breath I said, "If you think that I am going to waken my husband to go out onto the estate at this time of the morning to fight people that we don't even know, then you are very much mistaken. We moved over here a few months ago to start a new life. We don't even understand why the two sides fight, let alone want to be a part of it. If you want to get involved in all of this go ahead, but do not try and involve any of my family into it."

As I said all this I felt very brave but inside I was shaking like a leaf. I felt really sick, and very vulnerable there, voicing my opinion. The hood looked at me with contempt, and turning his back to me muttered under his breath, "You'll be sorry. They won't like this."

'They' being the rest of the hoodlums that were organising the comings and goings of the estate. I quickly shut the door and ran into my lounge, shaking. I lit a cigarette, and then promptly burst into tears. I was so scared. Now I felt myself in an awful situation. Should I wake my husband to tell him what was going on, knowing that if I did, he would probably go outside, and kick the fuck out of the ones who scared his wife? Or should I just leave things as they stood and hope that he never gets to find out about my visitor? Or indeed would my visitor tell the relevant dickheads who were organising the trouble in the first place that Wayne wouldn't come out and join them, so they would get him anyway? My whole body shook with fear. One of my children appeared downstairs and must have heard me crying, for a little voice said, "What's wrong, mummy? Don't you feel very well?" "Nothing that a big cuddle won't make better," I answered. It was then that I decided that I wasn't going to wake Wayne up, and after tucking my son into bed once more, I climbed back into bed.

The following morning I told Wayne everything. He said that I should have woken him up, but he could understand why I didn't, as yes, he would most certainly have gone out to give them what for. When I went out later that day, it seemed everybody was involved. Even mums and small children were now barricading all exits, so no-one could get in or out of the estate. We decided that the best thing we could do would be to go back to the caravan as soon as possible and to leave these idiots to it. We packed the car up as quick as possible, and knowing that we couldn't get out the normal route, we drove to the back of the estate and across the fields to escape. The next few days passed as normal, and I kept in contact with my next door neighbour to keep a check on how things were back home. We watched on the news for any information regarding Drumcree, and quite often our estate was featured on it. Various cars were blown up, petrol bombs thrown at the police who tried to put a stop to the goings on and a few of our neighbours got arrested.

Seemingly the coward's way out, we did wait for the trouble to end before we returned home, and when we did, it was as if nothing had ever taken place. Nobody mentioned Drumcree, and life returned to normal, but it was a couple of days after we had returned that I had the shock of my life. I was in the lounge watching television, Wayne being at work, when the door knocked. My daughter Amanda answered it and shouted, "Mum, someone's at the door for you." I got up and walking through to the hall I said, "Who is it?" When she told me I wanted the ground to swallow me whole. There just walking into my kitchen was the hood who had scared me to death the previous week. I sent Amanda back into the lounge, and told her to stay there, while I made my way petrified into my own kitchen. I walked in and immediately a smiling face looks at me and says, "Hiya Jen. How are you? Did you have a good time at the caravan?" In amazement I replied that I was great and asked him how he was. It seemed so stupid to be having this conversation after all he had put me through previously, but I felt so scared that I just tried to act normally. Then to even more amazement he then pulls out a bag of sweets for all four of the kids. "Well Jen," he says. "Can't stop. Just a flying visit. People to see, places to go. You know how it is." And with that he gets up to go.

Having shut the front door after him I felt physically sick. I couldn't believe that this was the same person although I knew it was. We were back to being neighbours again – pals, not people on opposite sides. He had one set of values, and I had another. At the time we couldn't see eye to eye, but for now we were back to being respectful to one another, each knowing the other one's secret. The only difference was that he could accept the troubles and willingly want to be a part of them, where I wanted to live a peaceful life with my family without taking sides.

We eventually moved to a mixed estate, and we are now accepted for who we are, not what we are, and live a very peaceful life.

Jennifer

I'd never been happy with the B-Specials...

I felt they had a very poor reputation – a deservedly poor reputation. Then the Ulster Defence Regiment was formed, and I, with a lot of other people who had had some previous military service, thought that this was a way of contributing towards a settlement, then seen as a military settlement against terrorism. I was working full-time in the Civil Service when I joined, and living in Portadown. Living in Portadown was an interesting experience, because I was there during the Ulster Workers' Strike – a strike I didn't believe in because there was a power sharing executive at that stage which I was in support of. I was very unhappy about the situation of having to doff your cap to these people in balaclavas in order to get to work. Then when you got into work, these boys would come in and say, "You have to get out, because you shouldn't be here working." I was increasingly finding myself out of tune with the way people of my generation felt about politics and everything else. It seemed I was already going down a road of separation from the majority of people I lived and worked with. I felt that I was a bit 'out on a limb', but I continued to work with the UDR part-time.

There were some terrible guys in the UDR at that time, some of them I knew. They were involved with the Showband killings outside Lurgan. The Miami Showband.

I couldn't believe the people who were subsequently charged with that, because I thought they would have been the last people to have been terrorists. But there you are. In a way, I felt sorry for them because to me, they clearly had stayed where they were, whereas I had seemed to be moving along a different road. They got caught up in paramilitarism and all the worst aspects of that. The UDR began to change and people who shouldn't have been in it at all were clearly being weeded out. Life was made so uncomfortable for them and they left of their own volition, if they weren't found guilty of some offence and then forced out. It became a different organisation. There had been quite a number of Catholics in the UDR when I had joined, but unfortunately Catholics began to feel uneasy about it, and that might have been because of suggestions of collusion. I think it was more to do with the fact that they were being intimidated by republicans and the IRA at that stage. They probably had no option but to leave. There were Catholics there, and I have to say, I had a great deal of regard for them, because they were actually putting their lives on the line. Not just when they were wearing a uniform, but also when they were at home as well. I think that has got to be remembered.

Jim

I've been working in Belfast since 1997 as a medical practitioner...

dividing my time between general practice and some forensic police work. Being seen as a police surgeon and general practitioner combined attracted the attention of the prison authorities who needed to offer primary care in a prison setting. Since I was an experienced general practitioner and also had some skill in courtroom technique and dealing with the police and other prison authorities, I was approached about a year after I arrived to take up a temporary post at Maghaberry Prison.

It's the only prison in Northern Ireland I've worked in and I found the experience quite stunning. On the surface, the brief appeared to be one of primary care, or general practice, but in fact, the setting is so extraordinarily grim, and the system so rigid and unbending, that it actually makes things we find in general practice almost impossible to deliver in the prison setting. For example, it's impossible to have a confidential interview with a prisoner. There are always at least two prison officers in any room when you're examining or talking to a prisoner, and the time scale for consultations is rapid. There are no booked appointment times, so you may find on a Monday that fifty male prisoners turn up for a sick parade which is meant to take two hours. During that time you might be presented with problems as trivial as a prisoner wanting a paracetamol for a headache, or a chap who's seriously at risk of committing suicide, and needs a lot of discussion and careful monitoring.

So I felt it was very difficult to offer good quality medicine in the prison and I admire people who try to do so. I think anyone who is preparing to work in the prison system long-term needs to be able to draw on some sort of support from outside the prison system, because it's simply ghastly to work there. I only worked as a locum, so I only got my feet slightly wet, so to speak. I wasn't deeply involved in prison life. But when I went in, I took the attitude that I was like any other general practitioner, and although the conditions were very strange, this was my general practice patch, and these men were my patients, rather than prison inmates. For me, I was a doctor and not part of the system, but unfortunately, it's almost impossible to be working within the system and not to be viewed by inmates as part of it. I took my strength from trying to remain a doctor and view these men as patients, rather than inmates, or 'nuisances'. I tried to extend them the normal courtesies that I would in any general practice setting. But I hadn't enough spiritual strength to keep going. I was offered a position, and there was a point where I might have taken up a job there, but I don't feel that I have it within me to work in such a brutal setting. I didn't have enough of what it takes to keep being there without collapsing within. The most successful people do draw from spiritual strength.

At the moment, most of my general practice work is in republican West Belfast. Working in a place like that makes you realise what the political situation does to communities such as Poleglass and Twinbrook. A lot of people have asked me whether I feel intimidated in these places by having what appears to be an English accent. Actually I'm Australian, but culturally, and I suppose linguistically, I come across as British. I see it rather as an advantage not being part of a tribal, claustrophobic society where it sometimes seems that everyone has their face and kerbstones and chest and every other part of them painted either red, white and blue, or orange, white and green. Yet I also think that lots of people in Belfast manage to live without becoming part of the tensions that exist between the two communities.

My being in Poleglass and Twinbrook as against say, the Mount or whatever hardline East Belfast Protestant community you may think of, is purely an accidental thing – the result of meeting the right set of doctors. I'm not there because I have a political cause I want to champion. I see problems like poverty, cruelty, unkindness and brutality and it's just not possible to treat these things with conventional medicine, although doctors go to extraordinary lengths to do so. I feel there is too much reliance on pharmacology. Medicine here, as with a lot of other aspects of professional life, is traditional and conservative. Certainly if I compare my prescribing habits here in Belfast with those of East London, I can see a much wider range of drugs being used here, particularly psychotropic mental drugs.

When it comes down to it, what I see I suppose, is unhappy communities relying on tablets to deaden the pain.

Lea

For Both of You

You lived for 11 days after the bomb. They say your arms and legs fell off when you died. I was only 14 years old and very frightened. Frightened to look at your charred face, your badly swollen lips and eyes, the tubes in your throat. Amazingly I remember a few jokes you tried to tell before the end. I think you knew how very scared I was. The smell of burning flesh never really goes away. God, how you must have felt knowing that your own child, the little girl you used to hold in your arms, was now afraid to hug you, to even be left alone with you.

When you died I wasn't there. I was huddled up with your other children at home praying. It was a quarter past six in the morning. The dockers were all going to work. They walked past the house, tipped their hats and nodded sympathetically. Nobody said anything, but they knew anyway. The whole of Creggan seemed to know, seemed to have been waiting and praying with us.

I made a scene when they tried to take me in to see you in the coffin. I was at that age, afraid of death, afraid again to look at your face. My poor mother, she pleaded with me, "You have to say goodbye, love. You'll never forgive yourself if you don't. Your daddy's smiling now – he looks fine." She was right. I edged into the room holding tightly to someone's hand and you looked peaceful. Still burnt, not so much like a horror movie. Peaceful.

The rest of the wake was exhausting. They say you knew one half of Derry, and the other half knew you. You had a military funeral, the Chapel and the grounds were packed. The heavens opened up as your own flag, the one you so lovingly flew outside the house every Easter for twenty odd years to commemorate the Easter Rising, was now draped over the coffin. Even the British Army stopped to give you a salute. I remember wondering at the time how you would feel about that.

For days afterwards the same reporters who stayed in the house, who accepted your hospitality during the Civil Rights campaign, now tore our lives apart, invaded all our memories of you, ignored our grief. It was a long time afterwards when all the furore had died down that the reality sunk in. I didn't know that mum and Rosaleen found you at the bottom of a neighbour's garden, that you weren't making a bomb, but knew what was going on and went in to save the children. They died anyway.

When I myself married and had a family, I realised what it was like to bring up children without much support. It was then that I started to resent you, resent you for leaving my mum on her own most of the time. When Margaret had appendicitis, when anything went wrong, you were always at the Civil Rights office or with John Hume, making placards, protesting. Then you died and left her with eight children, five of us still very young.

I know you suffered the worst kind of pain in those 11 days before you died. Your name is still on posters, plaques, the 'Roll of Honour'. Mum lived for 24 years after you, reared a good family. She died a few days before your shared birthday. Her name is in our hearts. I hope you were there to meet her, to ease the pain after all these years.

I miss you both.

Kathleen

Waiting

We both knew that the waiting was over. There would be no more pretence, no more looking away.

Later, much later, we were lying together, breathing as one. My fingers were tracing your skin, learning, memorising.

I felt a deep, hairless groove. My fingers recoiled and then slowly retraced the contours of the groove.

"I was shot," you said, "30th January 1972."

I looked at you blankly. The date meant nothing to me.

"Bloody Sunday," you softly explained. I could smell the candles burning, hear the old women praying and crying. And the taste of blood, your own blood, and the smell of fear thick in your nostrils.

And where was l?

I was hiding on my own side of the fence, my eyes and ears closed. Not knowing, not wanting to know. Condoning. But you crossed over to me, and helped me pull down the fence that divided us.

Grace

The Peace People & Troubled Times

Folk often refer to the Peace People as a women's movement, but many, many men joined too. The last straw for people who abhorred what was happening in our country were the horrific deaths of the Maguire children.

We rushed to join the newly formed Peace People in droves and marched here and there all over the country. Buses took crowds of people from every district to meet at rallying points every Saturday. Our message to the men of violence was clear. We wanted to live in peace and we wanted a peaceful society for our children. Naively, we told ourselves that so many people marching must influence those who believed they were fighting some kind of war.

I worked in Belfast then and ran in panic from the office almost on a daily basis because of countless bombs and bomb scares, walked the feet off myself when public transport was suspended, and worried myself sick about the safety of my children. I hoped I was doing something in the Peace People to make the situation better.

Memories of the march on the Falls Road endure because we were attacked. An avalanche of stones, bottles and muck came at us. But it was pouring, and umbrellas saved the day, but some people were injured. The rallying point for that day was quickly changed from Casement Park to Musgrave Park. I shall always remember my friend saying, "It's every man for himself here," as she took off up the road at a rate of knots.

There was also a social side to the Peace People. A few of us formed a group called 'Funline', responsible for the entertainment side of the organisation. It was important that people from all communities could come together and enjoy company and fun with others as an outlet from the ghetto-like existence in which people were often forced to exist.

Jumble sales came under fundraising and other projects. It was a bit like a child asking, "What did you do in the war, mummy?" and you'd have to say, "I baked cakes for peace." Putting on a Christmas dinner followed by entertainment every year was just one of our efforts. Afterwards, we would look at badly swollen ankles, rub aching backs and swear, 'never again'. But that was only until the next event.

Two 'Funliners' delighted in writing what they called 'Wee Sketches' and roping in the rest of us to take part. The Wee Sketches written by Eileen Toner and Freda Lyness were a hoot. Freda once adapted the words of the song 'My Way' to suit our activities. We were her backing group. Even now when I meet people from the 70s and 80s, often they will say, "Those wee nights we had in the Peace House were great." It is surprising that at this period when no-go areas were in operation, bands of women crossed the divide and continued visiting each other wherever they lived.

Eventually I became editor of *Peace by Peace*, the official magazine of the Peace People. During my six years in this position, the work and opinions of a great number of people were showcased. *Along the Road to Peace* was a book of articles compiled to mark the Peace People's 15th anniversary.

Almost from day one, there were unfortunately fall-outs and disagreements in the organisation, usually involving the founders. At times bad feeling would target one or more individuals. After a really nasty experience in this regard and manifestation of some dreadful behaviour at the annual assembly of 1994, I resigned editorship. The people who started it and the masses who joined the Peace People were a diverse group of people and, under any circumstances, there was sure to be disagreements.

Peace and reconciliation organisations proliferated as offshoots from the initial Peace People and, in the end, I think that good must surely overcome evil. If anyone were to ask me, knowing what I know now, if I regret that I joined the Peace People, I would say, "No. Looking back, I did what I thought was right and I'd still do the same again."

Rhoda

Every time you went through the station door...

you knew anything could happen – a sniper could be anywhere. It's only natural, in police services all over the world, to expect trouble. It's not all sunshine; you're going to run into trouble some time, somewhere. Somebody's going to break the law – at a football match, anywhere at all. That's part of your duty. You're going to have demonstrations about various things from time to time and that has to be policed. You're bound to have outbursts from some members of the public about something. But to start shooting and ambushing police officers, which the IRA done, and setting bombs – that shouldn't be part of the situation at all.

There always has been trouble, even back when I joined in 1941. There's always been trouble, off and on – the changeover in 1920/21, plus in the 30s there was riots in Belfast. My uncle was an officer at that time. I always remember a photograph of him leading a baton charge through the streets. I had two uncles in the police service, both of them my father's brothers. One was still serving when I joined in 1941 and had been in the RIC as well and served in Dublin. Then in 1921, it changed over and the Royal Irish Constabulary became the Royal Ulster Constabulary. My father-in-law was also in the RIC and left when the force was changed, to do some farming. He was from farming stock. When my brother, who was ten years older than me, joined the police service, I began to get interested too. When he came home on leave, he would tell me all about it and encouraged me to think about joining. The pay was good compared to other jobs, so I did join. It was during the war, and so if you were in any of the security forces at all, you couldn't get out of the force until the war was over. When the war was over, I was quite happy to continue on and stayed until I retired.

Quite a few of my colleagues were Roman Catholic at that time. About one third of the force was Catholic then. There was no sectarian carry-on in the city of Derry at all until about 1968 when the odd civil rights march started. The marches usually ended up quiet, though there would be the odd bit of trouble. The real trouble started in the city on the 12th August 1969, when there was rioting because of the demonstration in the city at that time with the Apprentice Boys, which the civil rights crowd weren't too keen on. I was stationed in Omagh at the time. I was transferred out of Derry between 1967 and 1971.

I wasn't long back in the city, when a colleague and I were stalked one day. We were both in civilian clothes and had been returning from checking out the damage at a local bank in Waterloo Place to see if there was anything we could do in relation to diverting traffic. When we realised we were being stalked, we decided to walk into a corner store that had two entrances and exits. We went in the one end and were able to go out the other side. When I entered the store, there was this loud explosion, and I felt a massive jolt in my back. Obviously, I knew I had been shot at. Then there was a second explosion, and I was hit in the leg, but I was able to continue on through and out the other door and headed towards the police station. My colleague caught up with me and assisted me to the police station and got a car and took me direct to hospital where I spent three weeks. I was convalescing at home for seven months after that.

My family were pretty well grown-up when these things were happening. We had to learn to be very conscious of safety when going out in cars. We always had to check it to make sure there was no bomb attached to it. It cut down on our activities with regard to recreation, and we couldn't go out at night unless we knew exactly where we were going and were able to make sure it was safe enough. That spoiled some aspects of life for us. Even at night, when we were home, we were always safety-conscious. If a knock came to the door, we always had to make sure it was safe to open, and it spoiled a way of life that prior to 1969 had been open and casual. We could have went anywhere then – any pub, restaurant or hotel. We had to cut down on all these things. If you went out, you'd maybe go to the next provincial town, maybe twenty or thirty miles away to carry out your recreation. That was the set-up. Even now, years after, I still have that feeling. I don't go to certain places. I wouldn't go to various pubs in the city. I like a drink, but I wouldn't go out to the pubs to sit for a couple of hours. That's all cut out, even yet.

I look at myself as lucky. Quite a number of my colleagues were killed in similar carry-ons. My son joined the police as well, later; it didn't put him off. I didn't encourage him, because he had another good job at the time when he decided to have a career in the police service. My wife tried to dissuade him, but he joined, and he also got injured. Badly injured. As I say, I was lucky, because the injury I received was very close to the heart. When the bullet went into my back, it travelled upwards and came out at my upper back. The doctor told me I was a lucky man, because the type of bullet was a low velocity, and as it entered, it took the line of least resistance. It followed an easy course out through muscle, rather than through bone. He said, "You're very lucky. If it had gone straight through, you were gone." So that was my luck.

John

Cormac's Eyes

I met another man once with Cormac's eyes and said you're from Belfast, and he said, yeah, how did you know? I said your eyes, you've got Cormac's eyes. I didn't tell him the whole story. He might have been insulted about Cormac and his eyes.

Cormac told me when he was growing up on the Antrim Road, they used to have riots with the Prods for fun and one time him and his mate were running and took a wrong turn straight into a big crowd of Prods. Cormac managed to get up over a fence and as he slipped down the other side he watched one of the boys lift a breeze-block over his friend's legs. He told the story with a giggle – and his friend was 'alright' and so was Cormac. He was going with a Prod now and I always liked him with his bobbly hat sipping his pint and hunching his shoulders as he giggled. But just as the pint would rise to his lips, just before he gulped it, his eyes would dart from side to side.

Joe

Four Bombs

The third bomb I was close to was also in a pub. It was in the Club Bar, which is now the Elms, just down the road from Queen's University. It too was an attempt at mass murder, for again there was no warning.

That night the bar was packed with students celebrating their exam results. I was not in the bar. I had gone into the off-licence to buy cigarettes. I was in there about twenty seconds when there was a horrible crump, and the door leading from the bar flew open. I knew immediately that a bomb had exploded in the bar. For a few seconds there was a stunned silence, then screams of panic and terror. I felt sick.

The bomb had been placed under the telephone at one end of the long counter. The bombers dumped it there and walked out through the caged area outside, put there for security because the pub had already been attacked several times. The pub was crowded that night, also and the fact that it was crowded with young students of all denominations did not seem to worry the loyalist paramilitaries at all.

Two young men were killed and another had his legs blown off. I watched in horror as he was carried out by his friends and placed against the security grille outside to wait for an ambulance. I will never forget the sight of him, sitting there helpless with blood all over him. The dead were still inside.

Ambulances arrived from the City Hospital and took away terrified, bleeding youngsters. I wished the bombers could have seen the horror and panic they caused, but it probably wouldn't have worried them. They would doubtless have seen it as a good night's work since it had the exact effect intended. It was meant to kill and terrorise, and it did.

Jill

Just Another Old House

The phone rang insistently, at 6.00 am on a Thursday morning in Tighnabruaich, West Argyll. It could not possibly be for me. Could it?

We had left Carrickmore early the previous morning, before the village was awake. William, Shirley and I were en route for Loreto, to show William the school and the school to William, in the hope of getting him to work a little harder towards his potential scholarship award. We also planned to visit Katherine at St. Leonard's School and return after the weekend.

The news given over the phone by my calm and sensible brother-in-law, John McAusland, was that someone had set light to our house the night before. As one of our appointed key-holders, he had been called out by the police at 3.00 am, in time to see the fire brigade damping down what had been a spectacular blaze between 11.00 pm and 1.00 am.

The previous month had been a particularly tense period in our neighbourhood. For some time, convicted IRA prisoners, with the support of their sympathisers, had been conducting protests and campaigns, in an effort to persuade the political authorities to grant them prisoner-of-war status. Such status would give prisoners the right to free association within prisons, the right to wear their own clothes instead of prison uniform, the right to maintain their own organisation and discipline with separation from loyalist and non-terrorist prisoners.

The government's response was that they would not negotiate under duress, and that, in any event, the demands of the campaign were largely non-negotiable since the prisoners, in the main, had been convicted of appalling crimes in pursuit of their unacceptable political aims.

The penultimate protest had been that certain prisoners refused to wear prison clothes, or indeed any clothes other than prison blankets, refusing also to wash or to clean their cells. Further, they decorated the cell walls with their own excrement. This became known as the 'Dirty Protest' and by its reporting in the media it raised world-wide awareness of the republican prisoners. However, though it dragged on over many months, it did not alter the attitude of the prison authorities or their political masters. In March 1981, therefore, it was announced by the republican press office that a hunger strike would shortly start – one Bobby Sands having drawn the short straw or otherwise having volunteered to be the first to refuse food, with others joining in at intervals of a few days. The calculated effect was that the protest would end either in victory, as represented by a climbdown on the part of the prison authorities, or with prisoners dying in series, a few days apart from each other and roughly twenty to thirty days after each had joined the hunger strike.

Householders in Catholic areas, including Carrickmore, were 'advised' for the good of their continuing health to hang black flags from their windows while the hunger strike continued, the predominant material in use being plastic bin liners. Being at a little distance from the village, we were not so advised. However, while we endeavoured to continue with life as usual, we had gained an impression of embarrassment among our usually cheery and polite neighbours; loss of eye contact and the occasional furtive apology from those that we knew well – "I don't agree with the black flags, but we were warned it was better to put them up."

It seemed obvious that the republican movement's aim was for some fresh martyrs for the ancient cause, to stir the hearts, minds and wallets of sympathisers around the world. Bobby Sands was buried on 7th May 1981, and rioters took to the streets everywhere in republican areas, in real or imagined excitement and anger. To one such group, it seemed a good idea to provoke a police response in Carrickmore by setting alight a large and convenient house that was lying empty for the time being.

On the Thursday morning, William and I somewhat despondently continued with our journey, while Shirley decided that she needed to see and protect whatever was left of our property, by flying home directly.

We had bought the house in 1972, calling it The Old Rectory in contrast to its earlier, grander names of Carrickmore House and Carrickmore Hall. It had been built in 1863, to the usual plan of an Irish country house, Georgian style; pretty well vernacular architecture throughout Ireland between 1790 and 1850. It may be considered to have represented an architectural hangover, being built in this style in 1863, by which time Victoria had been on the throne for a quarter of a century. Even in Ireland, linen manufacturers and others with new money and fashionable architects were escaping into new styles, such as Scotch Baronial, or were reviving older styles, such as Egyptian or Elizabethan. Such considerations had not had sufficient influence in rural Tyrone to cause the Stewart family to depart from the tried and tested Georgian pattern, albeit allied to Victorian methods and materials.

The names of the house's architect and builder are not recorded but they did a superb job of construction, using first-class materials and craftmanship. The walls were built in red brick, to a thickness of two feet, with an outer facing of cut limestone. The slates were Bangor blues, the chimneys lined with fireclay. Between the upstairs floorboards and the ceiling below, and within partitions dividing the upstairs rooms, heather and peat were packed as efficient sound-proofing. It was also an outstandingly dry house, which helped it to burn well when its time came to do so.

The Old Rectory sat on its own twenty acres, surrounded by beeches and Scots pines which had been planted when it was built. Facing south-east, it commanded a view almost without equal, even in Ireland, over a valley to Bernish Glen, directly south. By day, we heard the sound of curlews calling in the valley and often, by night, the screech of a vixen breaking the silence.

Marcus Gage, agent to the Stewart family in 1863, at which time the family were landlords to half of Tyrone, must have been disappointed when Sir John Stewart decided that Carrickmore Hall would be occupied by members of his own family and not by the Gages, for whom it had originally been intended. As the fortunes of the Stewart family declined in successive generations, the house passed to a Colonel Harry Alexander and thence was conveyed to the Church of Ireland to serve as the rectory of Termonmaguirke parish. Following the amalgamation of two parishes, a rectory of such size and style was no longer required. It was sold privately to friends of ours in 1967 at a knockdown price, on the implicit understanding that they would repair it and live in it long-term.

By 1972, they had had enough of living in Carrickmore, not least because they were running a business from the house and life had been made difficult by the recent destruction of the local telephone exchange. They offered the property to us, at what seemed a very reasonable price, and we took it. We were first-time buyers, leaving the family home in Omagh in which we had been tenants.

The only things surviving the blaze were remnants of silver cutlery and some bottles of wine. The first of these had been in the kitchen, at the farthest end of the house from the fire, while the wine had been in a small underground cellar, protected by a radiator that had fallen over it.

Post-fire experiences were full of interest. Our insurance cover was satisfactory, but complicated. So far as the contents were concerned, we were well protected by an inflation-linked, new-for-old policy, supported by an inventory and independent expert valuation, a rare piece of business-like behaviour on my part. The position relating to the house was more difficult. It is a principle of insurance that if you restore a damaged property you are covered up to the insured value. However, if you decide not to reinstate, as, within a week, we had decided, then only 'indemnity' or market value is paid by the insurer. The position was further complicated by the fact that while we were covered by commercial insurers, they in turn were indemnified by the Northern Ireland Office, but on a different basis to our cover.

Eventually, the derelict house and surrounding land were compulsorily purchased by the authorities. The walls were knocked down and the site was directly converted into a police fortress, which remains in place today.

Our story is but an inconsequential drop in the sea of misery that has flowed from Northern Ireland's troubles. No life was lost. No bone was broken. Only emotions and pride were hurt. We did not suffer, financially speaking; some may even consider that we benefited.

There are just two losers: the British taxpayer, who is well-used to such pain, and Ireland herself. Yet another fine old house has been wantonly destroyed, a concrete piece of social history put to the fire and a monstrous carbuncle of cement slab, steel and wire has replaced an elegant structure that had given shelter and pleasure to five generations. It still seems to be a pity. *Sunt lacrimae rerum.*

In August 1981, for a change, the Scott family holidayed in France.

Richard

Laying Down the Law

Among those stern faces, all unknown
to me that formed a human barricade
and claimed the right to peaceful
demonstration, on this occasion in
broad daylight outside the City Hall

By some historical impulse it seemed
realistic to assume that one such face
hidden from the light of the moon, may
have wore a mask the night before
in his quest for truth.

Administering justice, brutal, bloody
and raw; laying down the law in some
Housing Executive flat, implementing
the effectiveness of the Baseball Bat.

James

If I'd stayed in that area, I might have been something other than I am today...

I could just as easily have become a member of some loyalist group, but I didn't. I was born in 1938 in North Belfast, off the Oldpark Road, which then, was a predominantly Protestant area. As I grew up, whilst I was aware of people from another tradition who lived on the other side of the road, I had no contact with them at all in a social way. My opportunity to leave the area came when I passed the Qualifying Examinations, as it was called then – the Eleven Plus. My parents were happy for me to go to Methodist College which was on the other side of the town. More importantly, it supplied me with a very liberal education for those days. Still, although there were some catholics at Methody – as well as Jews, Asians and others – I really hadn't any close contact with Roman Catholics.

During sixth form, I took a job during the holidays in a wholesale chemist's in Belfast, and here I came across guys of the same age as me, 17 and a bit older, who were Roman Catholics. Although these guys were, in my view, both educationally and intellectually more superior than I was, they were doing a very low rated job on a full-time basis that I was simply doing to get me through the summer holidays. That impacted upon me. It impacted upon me, because this was my first encounter with people who were 'second-class citizens' in my community. All I had ever believed up until then was that if you were Protestant, you had a job as a right and that we were the masters. That was clearly how I and people of my generation were brought up, and we believed this to be correct and right.

After leaving school, I joined the army and that took me out of the province for nearly nine years and I came into contact with all sorts of different people. That widened my horizons in every way. There are only a few Protestants who still live in the Oldpark now, and they are the diehards. For them it's a territorial thing, 'Here we will stay', and it's not in their benefit at all. As for me, my roots never go down deep anywhere. I have a problem with the whole business of territory, because I think it's part of our problem here. We see the tribal signs wherever we go. I was born in North Belfast, but so what? It's an accident of birth, after all, where you're born. People will talk of sacred lands and about areas being sacred, but I have reservations about that. You go from there to becoming 'the chosen people', very quickly. I have problems with 'For God and Ulster', or 'For God and Ireland'. As a Christian, I don't see the connection between a country and a creator God. It doesn't do for me at all. I think you're better off not thinking in those terms, but people are what they are. If we would only think about where we are today, rather than continuously looking back, and saying 'this is where I was born'. If they could only see that, but it's a territorial thing.

Jim

I wouldn't wish to have been born anywhere else than West Belfast...

and personally feel grateful that I was visited by conflict on so many occasions, and have been given the benefit, first hand, of a lot of experiences. I used to ask the question, "Why me, Lord?" Now I answer that question by saying every event in my life has been an education and that has been used in turn to help other people, which is the most important thing about suffering.

But you don't stop being a victim. I've no problem with the term 'victim' and I've no problem with the word 'survivor', but you never stop being these things. Take Omagh. I wasn't there on that day. I didn't see a thing in Omagh, but I had my witness for myself in another time and another place. I saw a woman running round in circles, not knowing what to do, reaching out for someone, anyone. You saw people. You saw awful smoke. You could even smell it coming out of the TV. You could smell it. I had been there. I had witnessed. I had done it in another time and another place. That's when you become a victim again, 'til you get your thoughts gathered again, you can see yourself as that person who's running. You can see yourself in that situation, in that street and for a couple of hours you see yourself as a victim again. Then when you get your practical head on, you phone Omagh and all you can say at the time is, 'I'm sorry'. But you can't intrude on those people's grief, because you have to go through it as a community, on your own. Everybody ran to Omagh, and in a way that was wrong, because it disempowered the people of Omagh. Omagh should be left to grieve, then they'll be able to stretch out to other people. If everybody else would go and leave them alone and let them get that strength in themselves as we've all had to do. You have this strength in yourself. You have everything within yourself. But you can become a victim again when you look at such dreadful scenes as Omagh. But you pull round again and then you're a survivor.

If you live in this community and say you weren't affected, then you're telling lies – even the dogs of the street died. I saw two dogs lying dead on the street once after a bomb and two old ladies very distraught about the loss of their pets. You can't say you're not affected and you can't leave the past behind and just say that it didn't happen – because if it didn't happen we wouldn't be in this most awful bloody state that we're in now.

Mina

She was hoping it would be born on Christmas Day, her birthday...

We had five children then, and this was the sixth. She lived for the children and me and to have a nice house. She was very, very tidy and always had the kids' clothes sitting nice and neat on the top of the bed ready for them. It was her nature. She was like that always, even with my own clothes.

She'd been up early that morning. Around about 12 o'clock, I got up and looked around things and decided it was a fairly good day and decided to go out and draw some turf home, because the ground was dry. The kids were looking forward to going out too. That evening, she was feeling tired and she told me she was going to lie down for an hour or so, and I said okay, and was left to watch the kids. She said to wake her at eight o'clock and she'd bath the kids, but on that particular evening, for some reason, I just decided I would give them a good bath myself. When she got up, they were all in bed and she lined all the clothes up for them next morning because we'd planned to go away early. She loved to go away on a Sunday, whether it was a bad day or not. When she saw the kids in bed she thought this was great. She made a cup of tea and wasn't really in good form for chatting. She was seven months pregnant at the time. She said she was going to go back to bed. I remember looking at the clock and walking down through the hall and was saying I might go over to Greencastle for a while. This was about twenty past 11. Before I left, I asked her did she want a burger. She had a great fancy for burgers at that time. With expecting, she'd want some different thing. She liked a burger with a lemon on it. She said that night she didn't want one and had a drink of soda and water, baking soda mixed with water for the heartburn. I left it down in the room for her.

I went over and played a few games of pool with the brothers and some others in the bar. The sisters, at closing time, which was about half-one, were on about getting a carry-out and taking it back to their house which was down near the bar. I says no. I wasn't interested in that, but one of the sisters was insisting, so I says, "Okay, go ahead." I gave one of the brothers some money to get drink and the other brother was still there and I said to him, "I'll not be going down there. I'm going home." So I came on home.

We always put the lights off at night. Always. I thought I noticed the lights on when I was coming up the lane in the car. We never used the front door, except maybe at Christmas or some special occasion.

We always came round the back. I went round the back and switched off the car and went to the door and noticed that the glass was broken. I was just putting my key in to unlock it and started thinking that somebody had broken in. I met the kids coming through the hall to go into the kitchen and they were shouting, "Mummy's been shot." They were hysterical. I ran down after them and straight into our room and found her slumped over a chair by the bedside. She was still warm, the way I knew her. I remember hugging her, and feeling her pulse and knowing there was no life. I thought then about taking her straight to casualty and that she'd be okay. Then a terrible fear came over me and the kids were really hysterical, especially the young baby in the cot on the other side of the bed from her. He was on his hands and knees and past crying, just vibrating. I noticed all the bullet holes in the walls around his cot. I was wondering should I ring, or what should I do? With this fear, and the children screaming, I grabbed hold of the young baby out of the cot. We went up the hall and out through the back door. The bigger boys were still in their bare feet and pyjamas, shouting that the glass was cutting them. I remember shouting at them not to worry about the glass, to get into the car and get out. I thought maybe they were still about. On reflection, if they had been, I wouldn't be around right now. I remember driving very fast back towards the bar I had come from, because as well as being a publican, he owned an undertaking business. I would have got some advice on the steps to take. I remember all the lights being off around the countryside and the kids shouting at me for going so fast. Their heads were bouncing on the roof, so I tried to slow down a bit.

I got into the bar and the barman came forward and asked me what was wrong and I said that Kathleen had been shot dead. He put his hand on his head and didn't know what to say. He turned away, turned back and took me into this wee back room where a kettle was already boiled. He give me a cup of tea that was probably laid out for himself or one of the staff and said, "Give me that again."

The IRA have been accused of many atrocities, but I don't think I can recall any case where they went into anyone's house, and, when the intended victim wasn't there, shot somebody else, let alone a wife who was expecting. Had they gone for me, people could have accepted it. 'This man's served some time.' We often talked about the possibility of something happening to me. She often used to ask, "If they came to get you, would they kill me too?"

She had wanted a girl and had said if she didn't have a girl, she'd just have seven boys – a seventh son of a seventh son. Funny, she always talked about that. She was always inclined, at least once a year, to visit a clairvoyant. She loved talking to me about all he'd told her. She never once said he ever mentioned her being killed.

For a week or so afterwards, I kept thinking she would come back. I can see that in the kids sometimes. They think that mummy will be back soon. After a week or so, I caught myself on and said, "This is the end, she's never coming back."

Paddy

from

Devices of Detachment

In the end it all comes down to this:
the north of Ireland is a tiny place
and if someone's killed – and I don't care by who –
the whole thing happens right in front of you.
To step around it is a choice that's made.
We take the scenic route among the dead.

Damian

Extract of verse from BBC documentary, 'Devices of Detachment'.

The Lurgan Bomb

We were lying sleeping in our terraced house in Victoria Street, Lurgan, when this terrifying explosion jolted us out of bed. Our baby, who was a few months old at the time and asleep in his cradle, was distraught with fear.

Next, all the shop alarms facing our house were set off and this deafening noise continued. In all our bewilderment, we really thought the bomb had went off beside us, but it turned out it was the centre of the town which was devastated.

Eventually Patrick and Jonathan went back to sleep, but I was shaking with fear. Fear for anyone who could have been hurt or killed, but also fear that someone would be shot very soon as a reprisal. The old tit-for-tat mentality of Northern Ireland terrorists.

I sat and looked out of my window for what must have been the remainder of the night. Then, at one stage, I looked down onto the footpath below and I could see three or four silhouetted figures seemingly staring into my living room. It was then that I flipped. I ran over to Patrick who was lying in bed and squealed that someone was coming into our house and he'd better hide in the attic. He thought I'd lost my marbles! Maybe I did – for that short while anyway. I'll never forget the fear in my heart. I nearly collapsed with fright. Just imagine how a person feels in that split second when they realise that a gunman is running up their stairs and there is no getting away.

Mairead

A Letter

Cyril Murray was a singularly dedicated teacher, so committed to his work in Holy Cross Primary School that it led eventually to a nervous breakdown. He had to retire on health grounds at the age of 50. From shunning company, even friends, he gradually recovered a measure of confidence sufficient to allow him to appear in the staff-room at a function organised in his honour. We were greatly encouraged by this, and urged him to renew contacts with us all. He appeared willing to try again.

A few months later he was dead, murdered by the UVF who mistook him for someone else. A further tragic twist was that he and his sister who lived in the same house were within days of moving to Randalstown to live.

I felt – still feel – deeply the cruel injustice of his death, more poignant because of the kind of man he was. The poem was written some years ago but I do not feel the need to add to it. Perhaps you will accept it as my tribute to an honoured colleague.

Extract from a letter to An Crann which accompanied the poem, 'In Memory of Cyril Murray'

In Memory of Cyril Murray

Something of the darkness you'd lately
pulled yourself out from, shadowed
your eyes that day, yet your wit,
still keen, punctured our best speeches.

Beneath our staff-room banter though,
a sense of loss. Committed teacher
whom commitments drained, too late
we saw that we had not been

vigilant enough; now your retirement
and our rush of tributes, telling
you nothing you did not know
but never sought to advertise.

I phrased my wish for you in Irish,
I remember, to end my speech.
Go raibh blianta sona romhat –
May the years ahead be happy.

Just that – there were no intimations
that your future would be other
than we reckoned it. We pictured you
footloose in fragrant places around

Donegal, your easel in the heather,
your eye relishing the light
breaking through the cloud round Errigal:
and you'd have music near, a tape

of Mozart, maybe, delicate
in the mountain air…
unreal, unreal! All our goodwill
powerless to fend off terror,

your innocence no shield as killers
tore through your home one midnight,
mounted the stairs and found you
wide-eyed at your bedroom door.

Tom

I really believe that I had the best mother in the world...

She wasn't bigoted in any way. She was very much for the underdog. If she thought anyone was taking advantage of another person, she'd have got really angry. The night before it happened, or a couple of nights before, she'd been crying because Catholics were being burnt out of their homes. I must take after her, because I'm not against Catholics in any way, not even for what happened to my mother. But Sinn Féin, the IRA: I really resent them, though I couldn't say that I hate them.

She was a lovely looking woman my mother. Her skin was absolutely beautiful. She had beautiful skin and lovely hair. She had a great sense of humour as well. With my mother it was endless humour. The way she put expressions on her face. The things that she said. She was just wonderful. She was a very God-fearing person too – never would go to sleep without saying her prayers.

It was ten to six the day it happened. She'd been standing at the door, watching for me coming home from work. I worked in the bakery, and because it was just after the July holidays we had a lot of orders to do, that type of thing. I absolutely loved the job, packing and different things like that. There was one person who was always very slow, she just couldn't go fast. To be quite honest, I think she probably was – it's awful to say – but I think she

probably was maybe – it's wrong to say – too old for the job. She certainly wasn't fast at any job she was doing. But she was a lovely wee woman, and I hate saying that about her – that she was too old.

Anyway, we all had to stay late to finish off her job, and that was one of the reasons why I was getting home late. But also, the phone call made me late. The person who'd phoned my work, instead of saying to the person that had taken the call, "May I speak to a supervisor?" who could have told me what had happened and got me home quickly, he just said, "Can I speak to Jean McIntyre?" The phone was a long way from where I worked. You had to go a long way. When I say a long way, it was a few minutes from where I worked to the office where the phone was. The person hadn't told the supervisor the reason for the phone call. The supervisor had met another supervisor on the way, so they were just dilly-dallying, talking away. This is precious minutes when you think of it. Whenever he got to me and said, "Jean, there's a phone call for you," I had to get to the phone. This was all wasting time. I ran out, and when I answered the phone, the voice said, "Hello. Will you come home?" When I asked why, the voice said, "I think your mother's been shot." All these minutes were wasted. I came out of the office and I was screaming. I said to Bob, "Can you take me home – my mother's been shot."

It was a lovely summer's evening – it was actually like an Indian summer. It was so beautiful. Bob brought me up. It wasn't that far from the bakery, I actually would have been quicker running up. I don't even remember leaving him.

When I got out of the car, there were crowds around the door, and they were just hurrying my mother away on the stretcher, and she was obviously dead. She was killed instantly. I just remember holding on to the hedge and screaming, "No" and that's all I remember. There were people talking to me and I could hear their voices and I had to open my eyes to see who they were. They were trying to give me tea and I was afraid they were putting something in my tea to knock me out. I wouldn't take the tea or anything else.

My mind was haywire. I couldn't focus on any one thing, all I could think about was my mother. It was so dreadful, the most awful feeling – the most awful feeling I've ever had. My sisters and my brother came with some policemen and I really knew what hope was for a second, because one of the policemen saw me being comforted by one of the neighbours and told me the ambulance had gone to the hospital or the morgue or whatever and one of the police officers had gone to see what the situation was. For that split-second, I thought, 'Maybe she's not dead.' I had gone from devastation to that feeling that she might not be dead, just for a split-second. And then I turned around to the neighbour and I said, "She is, isn't she?" and she just shook her head. I was so angry with the policeman, I was so angry with the woman at work. I was angry with the person who made the call. I was angry with myself for going to work that day.

I was numb for months. When I went out, it was as if I were invisible. I was just walking around, and I was so sure that nobody could see me, that people were just walking past me and I wasn't there. I just felt that I wasn't living and it was the most awful feeling. All I wanted was to be alone with my mother. We didn't even want her to be buried. She was taken to Roselawn and we didn't want her to go. My brother and I were trying to think of a way to keep her, and maybe bury her in the back garden so we'd have her near us.

She was more important to me than anybody. She was the most important person in my life at that time, and even though I feel this way, I can honestly say I don't hate those people who killed her. I really don't hate. There are times I think about them, and wonder if they knew what they had done. If they ever regretted it. If they ever asked God to forgive them, and maybe they have. I don't know who they are – I don't know who killed my mother and quite frankly, I don't care if I ever know who they are. But like I say, I don't hate them. I thank God that He hasn't really made me a bitter person. I criticise Sinn Féin, I criticise the IRA because they were the people responsible for my mother's death, but I can honestly put my hand on my heart and say that I don't hate them.

Jean

Good Friday

11th April 1998

On this day, known as Good Friday,
I will place an assortment of
flowers upon an altar
as a sign of peace.

Some simple token to express
forgiveness, that covers the
divide of years, tears, grief.
And should the seeds of such

an offering fall on a stony floor,
leave open a door or window that
with this season the sun will touch
the core of such a gift, and breathe

into its very soul a fragrance of
goodwill; a spirit of hope that
takes root, throughout this island:

starting this Easter time…
as the Third Day approaches.

James

The whole policing thing, I find extremely difficult...

and I think in some areas, it will be the straw that breaks the camel's back – particularly in West Belfast, Newry, South Armagh, parts of Tyrone, Derry possibly. It can't be sorted out. At the end of the day, we can look at international examples like South Africa, but to some extent we have to think of the realities of the North of Ireland. At the end of the day, I have difficulty with certain members of the RUC who were guilty of a 'shoot-to-kill' approach or had serious complaints made against them on a regular basis. But then again, you have to see it from their point of view. They might turn round and say, 'Here, I don't want the likes of x, y and z in the new police service.' How would the families of bereaved RUC people feel if they knew certain former IRA volunteers involved in killing their relatives were part of the new police force?

I myself wouldn't join any police service, in any country, in any state. We need a police service that's representative of all aspects of society we live in. Whether we're going to get that or whether we're going to have that forced on us, I don't know. I really don't know what way it's going to be sorted out, but it's going to have to reflect the very real difficulties faced by people who live in areas like West Belfast and other, inverted commas, Nationalist Areas, where people are sort of reluctant to ring the RUC about even ordinary things. Unfortunately, you have to do that sometimes. Maybe your car gets stolen, or something goes wrong with your car. For insurance reasons, you have to contact the police. Or if something happens to one of your kids, you have to contact the RUC. On the other hand, most of the people in the Protestant community see the police force as a legitimate service, so how do you balance that? It's a difficult one.

Sean

The Other Side of the Mirror

9th May 1997: step with me, if you dare, onto the flagstones before that well known haunt of homosexuals, the Parliament Bar, Belfast. You are now standing upon the self-same spot, where, not so very long ago that folk memory cannot still recall, righteous members of Ian Paisley's 'Save Ulster from Sodomy' campaign hectored and harassed people coming in and out of this noxious monument to the sins of the plain. (Sodomy, for the purposes of that particular hate campaign, being so defined as to exclude from opprobrium heterosexuals who use the same practice for birth-control or pleasure, or both.)

Imagine that you have now crossed the threshold of this awful place. You're standing in the doorway and nobody is taking any particular notice of you. It's a quiet Friday at a quiet time of year. About twenty-five customers are making the kind of hubbub that about twenty-five not yet inebriated customers would make in a space that is neither big, neither small. The evening is just gearing up. Cast your eyes about and you'll see me, the bald one leaning on the wall between the jukebox and the archway, drinking alone, dog-tired and overworked. I'm a student at Queen's and I've been pushing myself hard to keep up with assignments. What I ought to have done that evening is taken my own good advice, and gone for an early night, with relaxing bath. But I didn't. I was feeling cooped up and isolated, so I decided to take my tiredness out for a drink instead.

Although I lived not more than one minute's walk from the Elms, I decided not to go there. Why sit amongst teen-to-twenties, trend-conscious heterosexual students with whom I felt mostly out of sympathy, when I could sit with marginally older, to definitely crusty (my own age grade) homosexuals with whom I felt like one of the family? I also appreciated the 'local' atmosphere of the Parliament, so that's where I decided to take myself off to. Using my preferred method of transport, I walked, arriving at about 9.20p.m.

I've been inside now for about half-an-hour and am halfway through my second drink. When I've finished it I'm going to go home because I've discovered that I'm feeling grumpy as well as tired – not the best mood cocktail for a relaxed evening out in my own or anyone else's company.

Stand facing the pub's main door and look at the clock on the wall to your right. It's just coming up to ten to 10. There are only two or three minutes left before it happens, but I don't know that. I am not Obi Wan Kenobi. I cannot read the ether and divine that a murderous explosion of impotent little boy rage has already been parcel-wrapped and winging its way to a spot near me. I am just an ordinary Joe.

There are only a few seconds left now. I'm still hunched against the wall with my drink. The whole of my attention is focused on an area of polished wood just above the bar. The light that it reflects has carried me a million miles away to a land called Plenty of Sleep as I consider going home in a taxi, so as to avoid the Friday heaving throng outside the Bot. That is, more or less, where I was at, mind and body, when the first explosion happened.

I say 'explosion' because that is how it registered with me, and still does – as an almighty ear-splitting thundercrack. A noise so sudden and so gross and so loud that it constituted a violation in itself. Reaction to it was an instantaneous silence of such absoluteness that you could have heard two fingers parting to drop a pin. The world simply stopped turning.

Bodies simultaneously freeze and leap to primitive levels of alertness. Every mind in the room bounces about insanely, trying to figure why the bodies to which they should be attached have all but fled the arena. Two more shots happen, and the silence ends. Pure atavistic panic erupts. Screaming, yelling, crashing, banging, and noises of distress barely recognizable as human spew into the domestic space as everyone dives for cover in a 'me first, you last' stampede for survival.

Recall that when shot number one went off I was star-gazing and being tempted towards the taxi rank. On hearing this shot I had the kind of normal 'this side of the mirror' thought which is likely to get you killed in such a situation. I thought, 'This is a prank, isn't it? It must be somebody's birthday or something,' and felt the early stirrings of a nice social smile begin to form, so that I would be able to join in the fun. Only two fast shots later I felt convinced I was going to be murdered by someone who had come into the place to massacre queers. The intellectual foundation for such a high-minded course of action having already been laid by the Reverend Paisley and his various supporters.

Animal instinct took over and propelled me into a stump of corridor that I knew to hold the backdoor to the bar. I would definitely be able to get out that way. It was locked. I turned and barged into a toilet, which, naturally, created a cul-de-sac within a cul-de-sac. If someone was stalking the place bumping off faggots, then I was now caught like an animal in a trap, along with the other people who had also taken refuge in the same place. Maybe I would only get seriously injured. I scuttled into the toilet stall and locked the door, almost feeling the bullets hitting me as they came through the partition. Two or three other men were also hiding there. We looked at each other and had what felt like one thought, 'We are going to die together.' So we embraced.

Keen attention was paid to the noises coming to us from beyond our bolt-hole. A whole minute passed without sound of further mayhem. We began to hear voices firing orders and commands. Voices that sounded as if they belonged to the world of rationality and order from which we had just been yanked. Someone called that the police were on their way. The words felt like doves descending.

In the same moment that I felt safe again, I also understood that someone else must have been targeted. When I opened the door to the corridor, I found a dying man splayed across the portal. He lay on his back, his torso on a level with my feet, and his head lolled towards me. I recognised his face. Twenty minutes earlier I had noticed him because of the strength and grace with which he carried himself. His name, I was to learn, was Darren Bradshaw.

I could have said that when I opened the door I saw two people saving a man's life. But that would not be correct. The pallor of the fallen man was pale, grey, and lifeless beyond the shade of any malady that I had ever witnessed. A second's glance told me I was looking at someone very close to death. A friend of the dying man, a barman, knelt at his shoulder assisting a young woman (an off-duty nurse so it turned out), who was ministering as best she could. She was dressed smartly in a two piece suit. I let slip the door and backed into the toilet again.

A man I had been locked in the stall with, not realising what was going on, also tried to leave. As he pulled back the door and stopped to register the shock of what confronted him, I saw the dying man's face again. He seemed to be smiling. I don't know if he was, if smiling was his dying expression, but that is how it appeared to me. An enigmatic, knowing kind of smile that seemed to say, 'OK, I understand things now. So that's what it's all about.'

Soon an RUC officer was in the corridor, hands firmly on the safety-catch of his gun. He gazed down at Darren unflinchingly. His face and eyes were an absolute emotional blank. Naturally I have no idea what the officer was thinking or feeling in the moment that I passed in front of him, and I recognised at once that his posture must be part professionalism and part self-protection, but the ice-calmness of his demeanor contrasted so extremely with my own quaking state of frightened agitation that that moment persists as one of my strongest memories of these events.

I filed past the officer and gained the bar area. A few seconds later and I was outside on the forecourt, which had been cordoned off. The first thing that came to my ears was one of the customers saying, in great anxiety, that he wanted to get away quick because, "Suppose a camera crew turns up." Then, I felt contempt for him. I do not feel that way now. Now I respect his anxiety. There are many places in the UK where it can be very difficult to be known as gay. Northern Ireland has to be one of the most perilous.

A plain clothes officer approached me and took down my name and address and then I was free to go, along with about fifty per cent of the pub's customers, who had already run off into the night in the minutes before the police arrived, or, perhaps more pertinently, before a publicity-bearing film crew turned up. I walked in a homeward direction in a trance, seriously wondering if I was being stalked. Near the Town Hall I flagged down a cab and spent the night at a friend's talking and talking and talking myself back to 'this side of the mirror'.

To an outsider like me, Ulster has the feel of a place where 'things' do not pass unnoticed. Everybody seems to know people from several townlands. There's a kind of savvy whereby people quickly cotton on to events developing a hundred miles away. It's the kind of place where things tend to get whispered about.

I believe Darren Bradshaw was killed twice. Once by the INLA and once by the press. The INLA killed him physically. They shot him three times in the back while he stood at the bar, because, apparently they didn't like an off-duty RUC officer drinking on their turf. The second time was by journalists who did their damnedest to wipe him out socially by throwing his reputation into the grave with him.

Darren was murdered on a Friday and several pages of sleazy journalism appeared by the following Sunday. The substance of the articles was a litany of loose allegations concerning his personal life – of a sexual nature of course – printed before his body had time to get cold. How was such 'intelligence' gathered so quickly? As I say, things get whispered about the house.

Stephen

I never asked it,

the stark reminder yesterday

flashed on the screen,

of 72

the Claudy blasts

the Simmon's song that made me smart

written too soon, I'd felt, being so near.

It seemed a sacrilege to me, so young I was,

to enshrine the real into the myth

so soon

I could not heave my heart into my mouth

things were so raw

so shortly all alive and then just void.

My teenage heart shocked still

as on our country air the Motorman machinery moaned

and echoed on our peaceful world.

The mad machinery moaned,

and then the triple blasts.

I cried knowing something terrible had ripped the world.

Now

they commemorate and pray

historicise

propose a monument.

I still cannot heave the living scar to light

for it to breathe again

and become a monument to what?

these sad old things are best forgot.

Yet not forgot

are best to live the touch of human love in human hearts

they don't and won't make sense elsewhere

Ethna

Author's note: Operation Motorman took place at the same time. Troops went into Creggan in the city, and the sounds carried on the clear air.

There's a blindness, I think, about what has actually happened to people in this conflict...

People will often say to me that they're a three-day wonder. They're the focus of attention for three days in terms of the media and then forgotten. I'm conscious myself that there were instances which happened that I thought were utterly horrific. You'd think about those people for a few days and then ordinary life took over again. You didn't remember these people's needs at all. Or if you did, it was for a very short time. So that's one thing that struck me about coming to work here – the massive needs that people had and their need to be able to talk about what had happened to them. People feel very censored within some communities. They're also concerned to talk about things that might be painful for others also.

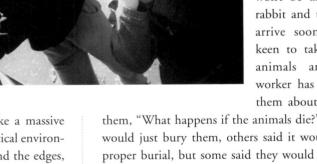

I often think of the troubles as being like a massive block of ice. If you like, the change in the political environment has caused the ice to melt slightly around the edges, which is where you find people are coming forward. But there's still a hardened core in the middle where people are caught in fear. Caught in terms of being concerned about what happens if they begin to talk about their experiences. What will it do? It's like opening the lid of Pandora's Box.

Bereavement comes to us all, but whenever it's as a result of the troubles, it's entirely different in terms of its severity and intensity and I think that's what makes it hard for people in the long term. In our new centre, we're hoping to have some animals for the young people. These are young people who themselves have been affected by the troubles, some of them have lost loved ones. There's a lot of discussion at the moment about what kind of animals they're going to have and one of them is very keen to have a horse, which sadly won't be arriving! But the rabbit and the hamster will arrive soon. They're very keen to take care of these animals and our youth worker has been talking to them about this. She asked them, "What happens if the animals die?" Some said they would just bury them, others said it would have to be a proper burial, but some said they would just throw them in the bin. That might seem flippant, but it's about how do you deal with loss. What do you do when someone very significant, someone you love dies?

Sandra

My mum loved to sew and she taught me how to sew as well...

and once in a blue moon we'd have gone up to the Shankill to look for material because it was always cheaper there than in the big shops. You could get a bargain. My dad always waited outside because you know what women are like in shops!

I can remember years ago, my dad, myself and my mum going up to the Shankill to shop. Because I was born in England, my accent was quite strong. Years ago, there was always this thing if you were English, people thought you were in the forces, which obviously in our case wasn't true. But I can always remember my dad saying to me, "Now, whatever you do, don't speak!" That was years ago. Obviously times have changed and it's good to see.

That Saturday morning, my mum and dad had decided to go to Belfast but I stayed at home. They had just bought a new house across the way and it was my first day on my own in what had been the family home. It was my first full day of independence. I could do what I wanted with no worries, without my mum coming in and saying, 'Don't do that' or 'I don't like that.' It was now a home of my own. I could stay up late if I wanted. It was a big thing for me. I'd been making a duvet and some curtains and wanted to put the curtains up to show my mum when she came home that day. Mum and I were like that. Even if she had made something, she'd have shown it to me, "Oh, what do you think?" You always got a sense of praise from her. Or sometimes she'd say, "You can sew better than that." But that's another story!

I was sitting on the floor in my own world with the TV on in the background. I think the *A-Team* or something stupid like that was on. The next minute the typical news bulletin came on. There had been a bomb explosion in Belfast and people were advised not to go into the area. Then they mentioned the Shankill Road, and I remembered then that mum and dad had gone to Belfast, but I thought they could have been anywhere in Belfast. I hoped they hadn't got caught up in it, thinking of the traffic. When a bomb goes off in Belfast, the traffic is horrendous.

Time wore on, and my mum had said to me she

wouldn't be long. She had so much to come back to, things to start in their new home. I put it to the back of my mind and got on with what I was doing, but I didn't feel right. I kept going to the window to see if I could see their car coming round. It went on like that for the next hour or so. Before I knew it, there was a knock at the door. It was a policeman. You know, living in Northern Ireland, when a policeman comes to your door you expect the worst. I knew that it was bad news. They had been caught up in it. He told me my father had been rushed to hospital and he was in a coma and he told me to get there as soon as possible. I kept asking him where was my mum. He kept saying my mum was with my dad. So I was left with this image, that my mum was holding my dad's hand, so everything mustn't be too bad, wasn't as bad as what I thought it would be.

When I got to the hospital my father had just died. My mother was nowhere to be found. Nobody knew where she was and that was the hardest thing. In a small room in a hospital, I said goodbye to my dad. I'll never forget the sight of him lying there, with his head all bandaged up and blood seeping onto the pillow. I held his hand and gently kissed him on the cheek. I told him how much I loved him, and said goodbye. That night, when I came back from the hospital, there was a light on in the house and I just knew that my mum had got back. It didn't dawn on me that the

house would be occupied by family and friends. She had been in the mortuary all that day and all that night. It just didn't hit me that my mum could have been dead all that time. What really got to me was not ever saying goodbye.

I sometimes picture my mum and dad standing there in that fish shop. I can actually tell you their every move. I'm convinced of it. There they are, two ordinary people, buying a piece of fish for the family's tea that night. I can picture my mum and dad standing there when the bomber comes in dressed in his uniform and this box of whatever it is. I can hear my mum saying to my father, "Come on George, get out of the way. Give that man room to get in there. Sorry about that." Because they were courteous. They were respectful people.

They said there was a warning shouted. There was no warning shouted. They didn't stand a chance.

The first Christmas I tried to get a headstone for my mum and dad's grave. They wouldn't let me put the words 'Shankill explosion' on it. They wouldn't let me put the cause of death on the headstone. Eventually, I was permitted to put 'Shankill tragedy' on the headstone, but that could be anything. That could be a car crash. That could be anything. They both died in an explosion. That's how they died.

Michelle

If we had went to Dunnes Stores...

we'd have been safe, but he left me to go to another shop. I presume he went to the electrical shop as he liked to look at electrical things. I told him I thought we'd better go out of the town, because there might be a bomb, but everyone thought it was a hoax. I felt very uneasy. We began making our way out of the town. I wanted to go get money out of the bank for Alan's new savings account and go to Dunnes Stores, which is a wee bit away from the town centre, and I said, "Alan, come on; we'll go to Dunnes Stores," and he says, "I don't want to go to Dunnes Stores today, mum." So I went into the fruit shop, and Alan says, "I'll see you, mum. I'm just going up here," and that was the last I saw Alan.

When the bomb went off, I was in the shop next door buying tomatoes. I had been feeling uneasy; something was telling me there was something wrong, and I was thinking, 'I'm going to get Alan and get out of here,' and at that, the bomb just went off, and I went into total shock. I knew I'd been hit in the head and thought I was dying when I saw the blood. Then I realised 'Alan isn't with me,' and I was scared. I took a bit of glass out of my head. It was a big bit, and the blood started to get worse. I had a white T-shirt on and a cream coat, and the white T-shirt was covered with blood. I went outside the shop and thought I would look for Alan, but I was scared, because I didn't know what I was going to find. Half of me wanted to find him, and half of me didn't; and I feel guilty about that, because I thought, if I loved him, I'd want to find him, and I do love him. I love him so much – but I just couldn't have seen my son like that. I staggered around and saw bits of bodies. I just couldn't look; it was so horrible. I didn't see anyone in the shop; it was just silence. I began to walk out and take the bit of glass out of my head, thinking, 'God, this is it, I'm dying.' When I got outside, I started to wander around and saw some people that I knew and asked if they'd seen Alan. They said, "No," and I thought, 'No matter how scared I am, I'm going to look for him.' A man asked me for my coat. My bank card was in my coat, because I'd put it in my pocket earlier. I took the bank card out of the pocket of my coat, because I thought, 'This isn't real. I'm going to the bank.' I gave him my coat and still had my bag over my shoulder and the tomatoes in my hand that I'd picked up as I gave the boy the money. I dropped them because I saw bits of flesh. I just dropped them with fright and started to walk up the way a bit. I didn't know at the time, but Alan was lying right across from me at the corner. He must have been coming to get me. The thing is, I feel as if he was trying to save me. Maybe another child would just have ran off round the corner, but he wouldn't have went without me. I know that. I didn't find him and feel angry about that sometimes, wishing I'd been with him when he died. Sometimes I'm glad I didn't find him, for if I had, I'd probably have ended up in a mental hospital. My eldest son and daughter identified Alan at the morgue and presumed he died outright by the look on his face.

Alan loved Celine Dion and we had one of her songs at his funeral called 'Fly'. The song was written in memory of her niece who died from cystic fibrosis, and it's about going beyond this life. The last line is, "Go now, find the light." It's a beautiful song. He loved the Titanic song as well. He was a very sensitive and emotional child, and Celine Dion is a very emotional singer. Alan and I went to see the film on the opening night. We couldn't get in to the first show, so he asked me to take him back the same night for the late show. We went and had something to eat. I had fish and chips and Alan had burgers and chips. He loved burgers. We went back and saw the film at the late show that same night. We didn't get a taxi home but walked. It was about one o'clock in the morning and February, and I thought, 'This is a perfect night, too perfect to last.' That night stands out in my mind, because all the other boys at the pictures were with their friends or their girlfriends, and he was not one bit embarrassed to be with his mum. He was really special. That night stands out, and that song, 'My Heart Will Go On'. It's as if he's sending a message to me, and the words in it carry me through.

I don't like to think bad things happen so good can come out of them, because that doesn't make sense, but I am led to believe all experiences, even bad ones can be used for good. I do believe very much in life after death and that Alan's just passed on to another life. I know deep down that's true and that he lives on, but it's still hard to be without him here.

Marion

You think you've all the time in the world...

but nobody knows what's round the corner. We'd just bought a new house. Colm had just started working in the civil service and was enjoying his new job. We'd just been married five years and had no children. You think you've plenty of time, but it wasn't to be.

It was a lovely summer's night in June 1976, and it was coming up on eight o'clock. We'd just finished our dinner. We'd been trying to do the house up, and Colm was going to do some painting and decorating. There was a knock at the door and Colm went down to answer it. The gunmen burst in and shot him in the hallway. I just heard the bangs and then the footsteps running away. After that, there was just silence. It's the footsteps you always hear. That's what sticks in your mind. He died after he got to the hospital, but the police had him dead before he even got to the hospital. They were saying, "What age *was* your husband?" and he was still alive.

I lost a year of my life after that. I don't know what happened in that year at all. My youngest uncle, when I started going out with John said, "I'm glad to see you're back with us." You don't realise it, but you must be away off somewhere in a wee world of your own.

At times it seems as if my husband has never been and as if, even in death, there's a hierarchy of grief, and people like myself are in the very lowest level. Because you're an ordinary Catholic or an ordinary Protestant, you don't count. No-one remembers my husband; no-one remembers what has happened to him. It's as if he was never born, because he wasn't a high profile person, or he wasn't maybe an RUC man or a soldier or a judge or a lawyer or something like that. He was just my husband. It's hard enough coping with the loss and loneliness, but when you feel you don't count, that's even worse. You have a pain there, and that takes a long time to go.

It's 23 years now, but I can still hear the footsteps.

Christine

The Callous Tide

Studying beside the scene,
passing the memorial each morning,
programmed into feeling numb.
It comes in surges
nobody knows when.

I remember the tide came into my town once.
I heard the famous people say so on television.
It was very loud. We all heard it crash against the rocks
  on shore.
It was very strong, because it took some people with it.
They never came back.
The water was too deep – it had been rising for years.
We were left sitting on the sand.

The 'grown ups' despaired at the wreckage left behind.
They knew more about it than me.
I was eight and didn't understand.
It never came back to my town again.

The ripples have now returned to the water.
We are all a lot older.
The water looks enticing and serene.
I wonder if it's full of remorse?
Surely it is not trying to justify itself? Yes, we are all a
  lot older now.
But I will never understand.

Joan

When they found his body, I said to my family, "I told you he was dead"...

I'd known it in my heart. Such a feeling of peace came over me that day, that he wasn't suffering any more.

It had been Palm Sunday. I'd been out at a Presbyterian church with a woman whose brother had also disappeared and we'd been sharing our story. When I got home, my husband said that someone had been at the house, wanting to know if Gerry Adams could come to the house later that day. I couldn't think what he wanted and the last thing on my mind was that we were going to get Brian. I couldn't believe it when he came and that's what he said. "You're going to get Brian back." He told us not to say anything until the IRA had made their statement the next day.

Brian's body had been found along with John McClory's, who'd also been involved with the robbery and disappeared at the same time as Brian. I'd always knew over those 21 years they'd be buried together, for they wouldn't have gone to the bother of digging two graves. It was a shallow grave in County Monaghan and their bodies were covered with heavy rocks and stones with two foot of soil on top of them. We go there every week now. The garda have put a big rock up to mark the spot where they were buried and we have flowers and photographs of them there to keep it nice. The man that owns the property says that it'll never be touched. It'll always be there for us.

Now, when I waken in the morning, my first thought isn't, 'God, I wonder if this will be the day that will bring something.' Twenty-one years that went on for. It was your last thought at night and your first thought in the morning, thinking of what his last moments were and did he know he was going to die? I know now that he must have known. They found him with his hands tied behind his back and he was shot in the head. The other night there was a programme on the television about animals and there was a sick horse in it that wasn't going to get better. The next thing you heard was they shot the horse in the head and it just devastated me. I suppose I'll have these thoughts now for the rest of my life.

After he was found, I had to go to the coroner to identify his clothes, and there was his wee jacket. He had that leather jacket on the morning he was going out. There it was. They had pieced it all together. It was all flattened out. And his wee watch and shoes. It just devastated me. You could have worn the shoes, they were so well preserved. There was wee bits of clay on them which must have gathered over the years but they looked the same with the wee navy stripes up the side. The garda, I suppose, had all the heavy muck and soil taken off them.

One of the things that had worried me over the years was how they would know the body was Brian's? Then they got DNA testing done and they assured me that even if it was another forty years down the line Brian was found, they would know it was him. Whenever he was found and I knew him and John were buried together, I just wanted Brian. I kept explaining that Brian was small, so that the bones they found of him would be small whereas John McClory's would be bigger. I nearly wanted to go down there and find him myself, but the coroner reassured me it was Brian. He's buried at Milltown now. When they lowered his coffin into the grave that day, I really broke down. I just looked into the ground and it was so very final.

I know now there is a God. He's made that known to me. I know also when you die, that's not the end of you. That's not the end. You're always there, and Brian's here with me now and so is God, more than ever. It has given me the greatest strength and a new faith.

I know in my heart, there is something very powerful, but then again, I can't understand why we were made to suffer for so long. That's something I would want to know – and why at the end I have to be grateful for being able to go to my son's grave. Imagine having to be grateful for that?

Margaret

when the UDA began to grow in influence and the Protestant population became increasingly threatened by the IRA attacks on economic targets – Catholic families and their property were going to be attacked. Most of the businesses and commerce, with the exceptions of pubs and bookies were in the hands of the Protestant population. The pubs and bookies went first, then homes and people were attacked. This was the classic tactic. It had been used successfully on a number of occasions and it served two functions. One, it stopped the spread of the Catholic population and two, it stunted their economic development.

When the troubles broke out again in 1969, I was married with a young family and living in the Ballysillan. People were frightened of the troubles spreading throughout the whole city. Vigilante groups were formed and began patrolling the streets. Their aim was to keep trouble out and everyone informed of recent developments. In fact, it allowed people to believe they were doing something useful. Catholics and Protestants patrolled together, although there were only a few Catholic families in our area. A lady at the bottom of our street made tea and sandwiches for the vigilantes. She was a very pleasant lady. She told me there were six Catholic families in our street, which was news to me. She also stressed her concern for their safety. She didn't know I was one of those families. The first cold chill ran down my spine. I didn't tell my wife of my concerns, but I tried to get her used to the idea of moving. She loved the house. She felt comfortable with our neighbours and wouldn't consider for a second leaving. As the troubles developed, Catholics were excluded from 'vigilanteing'. We weren't told we couldn't participate. We were just ignored.

When unionist politicians demanded the dismantling of the barricades, and the opening up of the no-go nationalist areas, the UDA lent muscle to their demands. The UDA set up their own barricades and threatened to set up no-go areas of their own. Catholic families behind these barricades felt like hostages. As the incidents of intimidation increased, the strains became almost unbearable. Sleeping, working, travelling to and from work with the constant worry for the safety of the family.

Explosives were found on a waste ground behind a pub

Anyone with even a basic knowledge of Irish history knew what was going to happen...

managed by one of our neighbours. The report on TV news gave the impression the explosives were found on the premises. That night a pipe bomb was thrown at the back window of his house. Fortunately it hit the wall above the window and exploded in the yard. Considerable damage was done to the rear of the house. I warned my wife to stay at home, and ran to offer my assistance. As I was standing in their hall, my neighbour went to ring the police. The first IRA truce was to end at midnight that very day. Two armed men ran into the house. One went into the living room and the other stood with me in the hall. He looked at his watch.

"Five past midnight. It didn't take the IRA long starting."

"Do you think the IRA did this?"

He raised his gun.

"Do you think they didn't?"

Then the other vigilante ran back into the hall.

"Fuck – this is a fenian house."

They both looked at me, then turned and ran out of the house. They were vigilantes, but they were armed.

When the police eventually arrived, I gave them a description of the two men.

"Oh, we know who they are. They're all right."

"How could they be all right? They're vigilantes, and they're armed."

The police knew there were armed men patrolling the streets. The second cold chill ran down my spine. A mob began to gather in front of the house. They were calling insults and accusing us of making bombs in the house. I pointed out to one of the policemen that the earlier news bulletin was partly responsible for this mob's anger and also, they were making no attempt to disperse the mob. In fact, one officer was sharing a humorous conversation with one of the most vociferous of the intimidators. Their response was, 'We're not the newsreaders.'

"But you supply the information, therefore you're responsible for this attack."

I was beginning to annoy him. He turned, punched me on the chest, "If you don't shut up, we'll take you with us." It was clear we couldn't expect much help from the police. A third cold chill ran down my spine.

My wife still resisted any discussion about leaving. A few days later, she went to the bus stop to collect the boys coming from school. When she arrived, a gang had the boys surrounded. They were armed with clubs. Luckily our boys didn't know what religion they were. My wife arrived just in the nick of time. When I came home from work, she was in a bad state. The police had been at the house looking for me. She thought I was going to be interned. It was a bad day for her. That was the first time she realised the danger we were in. "We're going to have to leave here," I told her. She loved that house. Really loved it. There was a garden in the back and there was a garden in the front. It was a lovely house. She loved it and we were happy there.

James

A lack of imagination in Protestant people makes me weary...

but there's a lack of imagination all round. A lack of imagination about how effective the church could be if it got its act together and a lack of imagination on how to express our identity in other ways.

What angers me about the divisions here is the way we have managed to set against each other communities which suffer from unemployment when, in fact, they share the same stories. I think therefore, it's very important in working-class or underclass areas or whatever you want to call them, that people be given the privilege of telling one another their stories. I think that makes a world of difference. Instead, the whole political thing gets played out in those communities. For example, there's a lot of redevelopment going on up at Tiger's Bay and they've built a new factory as a result of the redevelopment. One of the biggest negotiating points in the building of the new factory was which direction the door would face. Would it face over the New Lodge, which would make it easier for Catholics to come into that factory to work, or would it face into Tiger's Bay, which would make it easier for Protestants

to come into work? So, despite the shared story, there's still the attitude – we'd better not let go of our own, just in case. You never know. I would have heard that from the Protestant community. I don't know the Catholic story on that particular venture, but on the loyalist side, that certainly was one of the big issues. Sometimes I think, when it comes to Catholics and republicans in particular, we Protestants almost have a gene for suspicion.

For me, the Gospel stands starkly against that, not even against it but in contrast to it. God sent His son to die, not to hold His own, but to let it all go. So the Gospel says to win you have to lose. To live you have to die. As a minister, working in that kind of context, I would find myself wondering how on earth to express the Gospel to a culture that wants to keep for itself, hold on, win by winning. But it's a challenge that comes back to me. It's hard to get over what's been bred into you, so you need to always be aware that it's been bred into you, because if your first thing about people is to be suspicious of what they say, then actually you have little respect for them and their integrity.

I've never had any kind of formal structures for dealing with this – sometimes suspicion just really has to be lived through – and again, as I said before, this is where sharing the stories can help, because the stories also challenge. They can challenge our prejudice and they can challenge the collective memory of a culture, allowing a different story to come into people's consciousness. When I'm sitting in people's lounges and they tell me something, then I can share a different story in response and allow it to circulate around a bit. It's important to let the 'other side' in on the stories from your side. I've made it my business to tell a story to members of Sinn Féin, members of the SDLP, to members of the Catholic Church, local priests and what have you, so that they have some sense of the story that is being told about them. They have a responsibility to dispel myths as well.

The thing about living your life like this is that you never know if it's helping or not. I think that's something you just have to accept – that returns don't come tonight. They may come in another generation and they may never come at all. But the issue is not success. The issue is faithfulness, about opening up the complexities of life, rather than the black and whiteness of it all, for that's how people tend to see life here. In communities where you're split in two by a peace line, everything's either/or. You're either this or that.

For me the Gospel is about sharing. If I were to suggest opening up a church hall, giving it over say to a voluntary organisation because we weren't using it much, I don't think many people are committed to believing that this in itself is the Gospel. I think a lot of people believe you get people into the hall and you tell them the Gospel. But for me, the very sharing, be it stories or buildings, on an equal partnership basis in community life is living the Gospel. We have an image of our task as being message carriers, rather than story sharers.

Life doesn't centre around the church like it used to when I was a girl, so we in the church have to catch ourselves on, realise that things don't circle around us anymore and find some way of being significant in society. Unless ordinary people, as ordinary as me, are prepared to shift, then there's no hope at all. To do that, we need imagination, we need dreamers and I would say that North Belfast is one of the best places for finding people to dream with, to find all shades of opinion and all shades of approach to the church. I think North Belfast has been very downtrodden over the years. Downtrodden by violence and lack of resources and by splintered communities. But people are committed to making something different here and that's important, because if peace is going to work in Northern Ireland, it has to work in North Belfast.

Lesley

This poem arose at a moment of great intensity…

We knew that the tenth anniversary of the Enniskillen bombing would have to be marked. Some months prior to November 1997, I had commenced a series of conversations with a number of people, including principally those who were directly affected by the bombing. Through these discussions and conversations, we prepared the anniversary arrangements that would mark the tenth anniversary of the Enniskillen Remembrance day bombing.

All the preparations came together on the Thursday before the anniversary. In a moment of intensity, that was at times unbearable, I felt I wanted to write something down; so what I have written is not a crafted poem. It's not a manufactured poem. It's a poem that has emerged from a fairly emotional set of circumstances, and what I was very conscious of, was the tremendous intensity with which people who were affected by the bombing were still affected ten years on.

Over the previous nine anniversaries, the thing that somehow triggered for me the sadness of the Remembrance Day bombing was the falling leaves during the darker days of November. I knew this was the same for many of those who were directly involved as well. That's why the theme of the seasons comes through in the poem and the reference to nature. In the poem, nature reflects human experience.

So when I wrote about 'falling leaves reflect and move,/our tears,/falling on the inside./Hidden from the world', that was saying two things. It was saying that the falling leaves do actually remind us of the sadness and the tragedy and the losses of what happened in 1987. But also, that they're like tears, but the tears are falling on the inside, hidden from the world, because the rest of the world has moved on. Those who sorrow, sorrow alone or are 'Hidden from the world'.

The phrase 'Late Autumn, slow and dark/marks the end of summer/of the day the sun dipped below the/rim of our horizon' was again trying to convey the fact that this event had changed people's lives forever, in some cases tragically forever, by the fact that somebody near and dear to them was lost and never could be replaced. The utter sense of futility and the sense of no way back was a very powerful thing within the poem.

The early part of the poem definitely reflects what I felt was being experienced, and certainly what I was experiencing – the grief and the pain and the 'memories we dare not face/Of the end of the world, entombed in the rubble'. These were very real things that people were sharing with me and conveying to me and I felt they needed expressed. But the other thing I wanted to convey was the importance of hope in the midst of the tragedies of life. Whether it's the loss of a child through stillbirth or miscarriage, or the loss of a grandparent, or the loss of a parent, or whatever the case may be, that life will never be the same again. The world will never be the same again, and yet there is nonetheless a reason for hope. It had to convey that although the bomb had been an absolutely awful tragedy for so many, people had lived for ten years after this event and had somehow made something of life. To see people out for a walk, shopping, at a concert; to see people doing ordinary things – smiling, having a conversation, talking about things that had nothing to do with the bomb and that they had reclaimed their lives – I wanted to convey that in the middle of the poem, about time beginning again. I used the phrase 'A flickering Light lit a pathway, now and then/Where sometimes our feet could safely fall.' I deliberately put a capital 'L' at the word Light. In some ways, that was meant to impart the idea that for me; it was God who enabled people to walk again. I feel whatever the source of strength was for the individuals, the capital 'L' will mean whatever it means to the person who's been helped to get over those ten years.

The poem is entitled 'Redemption' and the idea for the title comes from two sources. There is the redemption that God gives us. We're redeemed, brought back from our wickedness and sinfulness. But there's also the redemption that we can create for each other. That's why, when I got to the end of the poem, I said 'Tell us you know our hurt that we/might reach to you/And ask of yours/And even think of hearing the voice of/Those who brought us sorrow.' The poem hopes for some kind of *rapprochement* or redemption between those who had been wounded and bereaved, and those responsible for their suffering. That would for me be an image I hold for Northern Ireland as a whole. There is a terrible conundrum whereby we need to have our own needs, our own hurts, understood and acknowledged before we can understand and acknowledge the hurts of others. When something happens to us that isn't acknowledged, then that in itself is a very painful thing. Now if we're all hurting, where does this process begin? There's no easy answer to that, but to some extent, we all need to be speaking and listening at the same time. For some it will be impossible; for some it will be impossible to speak and listen. There are some who would dearly love to meet those who pressed the button or pulled the trigger and to hear on a very human level what led them to do it. What were they thinking? How do they feel about it now? Would they do it again? If they would do it again, would knowing how much I have hurt make a difference? Those kinds of conversations are probably taking place in people's heads at the moment. I imagine there are people out there who have done terrible things and people to whom terrible things have been done who are having these conversations in their head already.

David

Redemption

A reflection on Enniskillen, ten years on, 8 November 1997.

The change of the hour reminds us
Of the day time stood still, and
The falling leaves reflect and move
Our tears,
Falling on the inside
hidden from the world.

Late autumn, slow and dark,
Marks the end of summer,
Of the day the sun dipped below the rim of our horizon.

Ten long years have passed.
Three thousand, six hundred and fifty-three days
Of longing grief and lonely pain.
So long for memories we dare not face,
Of the end of the world, entombed in the rubble.

Yet time began again,
more cautious this time.
A flickering Light lit a pathway, now and then,
Where sometimes our feet could safely fall.

Many hands waved us on.
Voices called to us.
We strove to fill the hearts of those
who wanted; needed us to walk again
In the sunshine of an uncertain spring.

We hurt still and it finds a fellow
In the homes and hearts of many.
Tell us you know our hurt, that we
Might reach to you
And ask of yours.
And even think of hearing the voice of
Those who brought us sorrow.

So, paid for us, we might find redemption
For the tragedy that has befallen us all.

David

Four Bombs

One other bomb affected me even more deeply, though indirectly. It was in the Rose & Crown Pub on the Lower Ormeau Road, only a few yards away from Sean Graham's bookmakers, where five people were brutally slaughtered. People remember Sean Graham's, but the Rose & Crown bomb seems to have been largely forgotten about, even though it killed six men. The reason I remember it is because one of them worked for my father-in-law. His name was Tommy.

Tommy lived nearby, and he survived just long enough to speak to his children. When they heard the explosion they rushed out of the house and round the corner to the pub. They found their father literally in bits lying on the floor. The bar was a scene of carnage.

Years later, by pure chance, I talked to one of the men involved in the Rose & Crown bombing. He was in the UVF and was still at school at the time. Later he was arrested and spent 12 years in the Maze Prison, Long Kesh. While he was in there, he met his republican counterparts for the first time and realised they were ordinary people like himself without horns and tails. For him it was a revelation.

I arranged to meet him for a project I was doing on children of the troubles, but at first I was reluctant to speak to him because of Tommy. I hadn't met him before and thought he would turn out to be some kind of brainless thug, but I was wrong. He was a quietly-spoken man in his thirties, articulate and highly intelligent.

He told me his life story, about growing up in a working-class Protestant area of Belfast. He joined the UVF as a teenager in the early 70s because he listened to certain unionist politicians and thought it was his duty to go out and do his bit for the loyalist cause.

When I ventured to ask him about the Rose & Crown, he said he was told it was "full of IRA men". Later, when he learned a bit of sense, he realised that the people who drank there were just ordinary working-class Catholics. Like Tommy.

Jill

It was decided we were going to go out and fire a few shots at an RUC man…

To me, this sounded pretty normal because it was happening all the time. I was 16, just turned 17 and at that time the conflict was really at a peak in a sense. It was a great time for us kids. I would have been involved in joy-riding; any devilment, you name it, and I was up to my neck in it. Whereas before, the excitement for kids, the big buzz, would have been smoking around corners or missing school. When the conflict started, that's where we got our buzz. Whole communities became involved and the common enemy was the RUC, Paisley and the Orangemen. I became involved more through peer pressure than republican politics. I had no real connection with the movement. I came in through the back door, so to speak, because of the action. Friends of mine that I grew up with and went to school with became involved with the republican movement and had access to weapons, which is a great bonus for a community. Anyone with a weapon has a real position of power. For me, it was a boost of self-esteem or something. You were part of a bigger thing and felt important. So it was decided, we were going to go out and fire a few shots at an RUC man. We went out, pulled up at a location, and shots were fired. I was sitting in the back of the car with fingers in my ears, frightened to death by these things exploding. After that, I was in at the deep end. In short, we were caught. This guy was killed. We were brought to court. I remember the judge saying, "Even though you didn't fire the shots, you're as guilty as those who did," so I was convicted, although in court, we were told to say that we refused to recognise this illegal assembly. Reflecting on that, it was a great buzz to turn around to the whole judiciary at the time, learned gentlemen and people with wisdom and the whole RUC and military and just dismiss them at the age of 17. At the same time, I felt like Oliver Twist, just repeating what I was told to say. It was also a lonely time. I always remember there was only one person in that court there for me, and that was my mother. I remember looking back into the gallery and she was standing there in a Belfast court on her own. It seems so unreal.

Because I had no real connection with the republican movement, I felt ostracised within that group. Although I felt like a republican and learned what a republican was through the years of imprisonment, my beliefs were more socialist. My mother would have been a real socialist. Through the ordinary politics of the day, we felt discriminated against in the ordinary things of life. We lived in a real poverty-stricken area where most of the priorities were on survival, just ordinary survival. Although the prison service became the common enemy when you were inside, some of my comrades were also the enemy, though they might never have been aware of this. The republicans kept the prisoners in place and you were dependent for your safety within the prison on the republican movement. People abused their power. Where there's power, there's corruption. In order to survive there, you had to shut yourself down emotionally. The first time I cried in prison was because I was frightened. I was on my own. I was young. I cried in my cell because outside the environment of the cell, in the wing, you didn't show that side of yourself because of the old macho image of having to be tough. The others couldn't stand anyone breaking down because it would trigger something in them as well. You had to be strong to get through the environment. I shut a lot of things down to cope and now unfortunately, I feel this has carried into the real world, because prison was a phony world.

I'm out 11 years now, but the strange thing is, I still feel like a prisoner – I feel it as fresh as the first day I got out. I was recently asked back to the prison to do a piece of counselling work, an introduction to counselling, so I walked back into the blocks as a teacher this time. It was unbelievable – I mean, I felt like a prisoner immediately. I actually followed the guard in front of me who was opening the gate as if I was back in prison. The group I was working with were all strangers to me, and so I tried to gain from them a knowledge of how they felt and what they thought and how they coped. I found that same system of shutting down. Emotions were shut. They'd rather talk about politics. They could talk about politics all day, but dare ask the question, "What do you feel right now?" and they deflected onto something else.

I picked up a book when I was in prison about the 1922 campaign and the cover was in Irish 'Was it worth a drop of blood?' That always sticks in my mind when I think of the people who died, the people whose lives have been destroyed. I wonder has it been worth a drop of blood? We got caught up in an old struggle, some romantic dream that's destroyed a generation. And for what purpose? Some good things about equality and justice have come out of it, but the impact has yet to be felt. I wonder, could there have been another way? It's frightening to think of the people who are dead. It's frightening to think of the lives that have been destroyed. I never really thought about the person who was killed because I didn't see anything. That was my defence in a sense. I didn't witness anyone being killed. It's like a reporter in the news. Someone has been shot. The criteria for release was that you show remorse and say you would never do it again. That was no problem. I didn't know the person who died. It was a uniformed person. In other words, I did what the prison officers were doing. I gave the person a uniform and he ceased to be a person. He ceased to be a human being.

If I had a chance to talk to some of those who've been hurt, I'd say what I'm saying now. This is me and this is what I thought at the time and this is how I feel now. Maybe they would attack me verbally or emotionally because of their loss and in doing that it would be therapeutic. But I wouldn't see myself meeting them for that purpose – to be a sounding board for their hatred. I just want to be me, for them to like or dislike me, and hear how I saw the world at that time.

Gerry

Bank Holiday Monday

I go down to the village by car to buy the *Irish Times*. After I leave the shop I see Paul in *Shadow IV* on the other side of the harbour. He sees me, waves – I wave back.

I'm reading the paper at the back of the cottage – it is a beautiful sunny day – when I hear the explosion. I think I know from the direction what it is. Then I'm running for the car. I tell my wife to stay in the cottage. I'm very apprehensive, scared. I drive very fast to where I know the boat should be. I stop at the cliff overlooking the sea. I see bits of wood moving outwards in roughly concentric circles from a churned up centre in the sea. I panic. I think no-one could have survived. I decide to swim out and dive in the hope of finding Paul's body. I'm stopped by a garda who tells me to go to the harbour. I do, by car.

Peter McHugh is in his boat. I ask him to take me out to the site. He takes me into the boat. There are two others in it. I explain about Paul. Nobody speaks. When we're clear of the harbour, we meet various boats coming in. I ask Peter to bring me to where the explosion occurred – he says it's too late and brings me back to the harbour. I'm annoyed he did not go further out, but realise he is right.

I see a motorised dingy with a bloodied Lord Brabourne lying in the back and others injured lying in the bottom of it. I can't believe this is happening. I don't see Paul anywhere. I think he may still be alive. I ran around asking people have they seen him. Nobody has. A man tells me that Paul has been brought in and that he is injured but alive in the Pier Head House. I am elated. I run in and am shown a fair-haired, badly-injured boy, who is not Paul. I feel destroyed.

I run out again and at the end of the harbour I meet Gus Mulligan who tells me Paul's dead body is in his boat. I jump aboard and find him in the bottom of the boat. I lift him in my arms and feel him limp. His back is uninjured and I recognise the large mole on it. I'm shocked that his back is warm. I rock back and forth with him. Then I feel an uncontrollable rage. I shout, I call the IRA cowards. I yell that Paul is as good an Irishman as anyone else. What political aim can be gained by killing your own people? I want those who did it to hear me – to confront them physically – maybe to kill them.

The anger suddenly leaves me and I feel the pain – the enormity of his death hits me. I feel it in my stomach. I feel utter desolation, loneliness. I'm thinking that nobody should ever feel like this. I've never experienced anything like it. The pain is not physical, so pain is maybe not the right word but what I feel is a pain of knowledge. A knowledge which tells me that Paul is suddenly dead forever. It is final. There is no going back to a few hours ago.

Now I become conscious that my reaction to Paul's death could lead to others suffering as I am, if I react in any way which invites retribution and I determine that I will try not to contribute in any way to this kind of action.

Jim Morrison arrives with a blanket and we wrap up Paul's body gently. It feels broken. Ambulance men come and put the body on a stretcher and as they bring it to the ambulance, I walk away feeling nihilistic and numb. There is no point in staying with his body. I wonder at myself doing this – it seems like desertion.

I wander about, among the crowds who have gathered. I meet a friend from Enniskillen who says, "Isn't it a nice day?" He has not heard what happened. I don't try to explain.

Jack McCarrol takes me in his car to the mortuary in Sligo to identify Paul's body. I do so and stay with him for a while and stroke his face and hair. His hair is sticky from sea water and there are little pock-marks on his face from the explosion. I feel overcome by sadness and love and when I leave I sit down and cry for a long time. I feel as though I can't stop.

Loss

For Paul who was killed, aged 15, by a bomb.

His death came,
like a door,
slammed.
Like a kick on the head.

I cried,
the sight of his body,
the little pock marks
on his face.

His still warm back,
negated his going,
so I asked again,
is he dead?

Now I grieve,
not for me,
but for
a perished potential.

He will not know physical fusion
ever.
The coalescence of love.

He will not know
procreation
ever.
The joystick of birth.

He will not know
others
ever.
The altruistic possibility.

He was born
tabula rasa.
The slate
was not half filled.

John

Future

The future is tomorrow,
soon or far away.
We can make history,
by what we do today.

Joanne, aged 15

List of Contributors

Adrian   Adrian Fox
Holiday Home, p. 77

Aisling   Aisling Hannaway
Before the Whole World Dies, p. 44

Anne   Anne Bodel
Token Gestures, p. 68

Billy   Billy Hutchinson
The difficulty was, everybody had been conditioned to believe...,
p. 25
I believe the way forward for this country ..., p. 50

Christine   Christine Huddlestone
You think you've all the time in the world ..., p. 118

Chun Kiu   Chun Kiu
My parents are originally from Hong Kong New Territories, p. 38

Damian   Damian Gorman
from *Devices of Detachment, p. 100*

David   David Bolton
This poem arose at a moment of great intensity, p. 126
Redemption, p. 128

David   David Robinson
Blue Shirts, Green Shirts, p. 51

Debbie   Debbie Caufield
Excommunicate, p. 15
The Orange Field, p. 66

Deirdre   Deirdre Starrs
Granny's House, p. 10

Dennis   Dennis Greig
Fifteen Lines for Omagh, p. 45

Dominic   Dominic Crichard
What type of people would have you beaten you off the road just so
they can march?..., p. 70

Enda   Wishes to use first name only
A Door on the Troubles, p. 20

Ethna   Ethna Johnston
Claudy, p. 112

Eva   Eva Bates
Footsteps, p. 60

Gerry   Gerry McClelland
It was decided we were going to go out and fire a few shots at an
RUC man ..., p. 130

George   Prefers to remain anonymous
My whole life changed ..., p. 22

Grace   Wishes to use first name only
Waiting, p. 86

Heather   Heather Newcombe
My Worst Nightmare, p. 30

Isabel   Isabel McGuinness
The Worst Day of My life, p. 8

Jack   Jack McErlean
Friday 7th April 1972, p. 57

An Invitation

An Crann *The Tree* has established an archive which houses the stories of conflict from the current troubles and other periods of conflict in Ireland within living memory. The archive is a unique and growing collection of personal testimony, reminiscence and insight, respecting the value and esteem we accord to individual experience and the diversity of response to those experiences. Contributions range from letters, diary extracts, poems, biographical sketches, factual accounts, taped interviews, photographs, drawings, paintings, songs, videos and music. Some contributors simply ask us to store their piece or artefact, while others give permission for their piece to be used publicly as part of a process that contributes to the building of a more inclusive story of our conflicts. It is An Crann's belief that only by encountering all perspectives can we as a society break through prejudice and suspicion to rediscover our similarities, respect our differences and chart a fresh future together.

If you would like to contribute something to the archive or have your story recorded by one of our experienced staff or volunteers, we will be delighted to hear from you. Dedicated to working inclusively and non-judgementally, your story will be treated with the highest regard and respect. Please contact us at the following address or telephone number if you would like to receive further information or talk to someone at our Belfast or Derry/ Londonderry office.

An Crann · The Tree
10 Arthur Street
Belfast BT1 4GD
Tel: 028 9024 0209
Fax: 028 9024 0219
e-mail: AnCrann1@compuserve.com